The Letters of Abelard

and Héloïse

by

Peter Abelard and Héloïse

D1114093

Published by
Feather Trail Press

Table of Contents

The tomb of Abelard and Héloïse in the cemetery of Père Lachaise, Paris.

Letter 1:

Abelard to Philintus

The last time we were together, Philintus, you gave me a melancholy account of your misfortunes; I was sensibly touched with the relation, and like a true friend bore a share in your griefs. What did I not say to stop your tears? I laid before you all the reasons philosophy could furnish, which I thought might anyways soften the strokes of fortune. But all these endeavours have proved useless; grief, I perceive, has wholly seized your spirits, and your prudence, far from assisting, seems to have forsaken you. But my skilful friendship has found out an expedient to relieve you. Attend to me a moment, hear but the story of my misfortunes, and yours, Philintus, will be nothing as compared with those of the loving and unhappy Abelard. Observe, I beseech you, at what expense I endeavour to serve you; and think this no small mark of my affection; for I am going to present you with the relation of such particulars as it is impossible for me to recollect without piercing my heart with the most sensible affliction. You know the place where I was born, but not, perhaps, that I was born with those complexional faults which strangers charge upon our nation—an extreme lightness of temper, and great inconstancy. I frankly own it, and shall be as free to acquaint you with those good qualities which were observed in me. I had a natural vivacity and aptness for all the polite arts. My father was a gentleman and a man of good parts; he loved the wars, but differed in his sentiments from many who follow that profession. He thought it no praise to be illiterate, but in the camp he knew how to converse at the same time with the Muses and Bellona. He was the same in the management of his family, and took equal care to form his children to the study of polite learning as to their military exercises. As I was his eldest, and consequently his favourite son, he took more than ordinary care of my education. I had a natural genius for study, and made extraordinary progress in it. Smitten with the love of books, and the praises which on all sides were bestowed upon me, I aspired to no other reputation than that of learning. To my brothers I leave the glory of battles and the pomp of triumphs; nay, more, I yielded them up my birthright and patrimony. I knew necessity was the great spur to study, and was afraid I should not merit the title of learned if I distinguished myself from others by nothing but a more plentiful fortune. Of all the sciences logic was the most to my taste. Such were the arms I chose to profess. Furnished with the weapons of reasoning I took pleasure in going to public disputations to win trophies; and wherever I heard that this art flourished, I ranged, like another Alexander, from province to province, to seek new adversaries with whom I might try my strength.

The ambition I had to become formidable in logic led me at last to Paris, the centre of politeness, and where the science I was so smitten with had usually been in the greatest perfection. I put myself under the direction of one Champeaux, a professor who had acquired the character of the most skilful philosopher of his age, but by negative excellencies only as being the least ignorant! He received me with great demonstrations of kindness, but I was not so happy as to please him long; for I was too knowing in the subjects he discoursed upon, and I often confuted his notions. Frequently in our disputations I pushed a good argument so home that all his subtlety was not able to elude its force. It was impossible he should see himself surpassed by his scholar without resentment. It is sometimes dangerous to have too much merit.

Envy increased against me in proportion to my reputation. My enemies endeavoured to interrupt my progress, but their malice only provoked my courage. Measuring my abilities by the jealousy I had raised, I thought I had no further need for Champeaux's lectures, but rather that I was sufficiently qualified to read to others. I stood for a post which was vacant at Melun. My master used all his artifice to defeat my hopes, but in vain; and on this occasion I triumphed over his cunning as before I had done over his learning. My lectures were always crowded, and my beginnings so fortunate, that I entirely obscured the renown of my famous master. Flushed with these happy conquests, I removed to Corbeil to attack the masters there, and so establish my character of the ablest logician. The rush of travelling threw me into a dangerous distemper, and not being able to recover my health, my physicians, who perhaps were in league with Champeaux, advised me to remove to my native air. Thus I voluntarily banished myself for some years. I leave you to imagine whether my absence was not regretted by the better sort. At length I recovered my health, when I received news that my greatest adversary had taken the habit of a monk; you may think it was an act of penitence for having persecuted me; quite the contrary, 'twas ambition; he resolved to raise himself to some church dignity, therefore fell into the beaten track and took on him the garb of feigned austerity; for this is the easiest and shortest way to the highest ecclesiastical dignities. His wishes were successful and he obtained a bishopric; yet did he not quit Paris and the care of his schools: he went to his diocese to gather in his revenues, but returned and passed the rest of his time in reading lectures to those few pupils which followed him. After this I often engaged with him, and may reply to you as Ajax did to the Greeks:—

'If you demand the fortune of that day
When stak'd on this right hand your honours lay,
If I did not oblige the foe to yield,
Yet did I never basely quit the field.'

About this time my father, Beranger, who to the age of sixty had lived very agreeably, retired from the world and shut himself up in a cloister, where he offered up to Heaven the languid remains of a life he could make no further use of. My mother, who was yet young, took the same resolution. She turned a Religious, but did not entirely abandon the satisfactions of life; her friends were continually at the grate, and the monastery, when one has an inclination to make it so, is exceedingly charming and pleasant. I was present when my mother was professed. At my return I resolved to study divinity, and inquired for a director in that study. I was recommended to one Anselm, the very oracle of his time, but, to give you my own opinion, one more venerable for his age and his wrinkles than for his genius or learning. If you consulted him upon any difficulty, the sure consequence was to be much more uncertain in the point. They who only saw him admired him, but those who reasoned with him were extremely dissatisfied. He was a great master of words and talked much, but meant nothing. His discourse was a fire, which, instead of enlightening, obscured everything with its smoke; a tree beautified with variety of leaves and branches, but barren of fruit. I came to him with a desire to learn, but found him like the fig tree in the Gospel, or the old oak to which Lucan compares Pompey. I continued not long underneath his shadow. I took for my guides the primitive Fathers and boldly launched into the ocean of the Holy Scriptures. In a short time I had made such progress that others chose me for their director. The number of my scholars was incredible, and the gratuities I received from them were proportionate to the great reputation I had acquired. Now I found myself safe in the harbour, the storms were passed, and the rage of my enemies had spent itself without effect. Happy had I known to make a right use of this calm! But when the mind is most easy 'tis most exposed to love, and even security is here the most dangerous state.

And now, my friend, I am going to expose to you all my weaknesses. All men, I believe, are under a necessity of paying tribute at some time or other to Love, and it is vain to strive to avoid it. I was a philosopher, yet this tyrant of the mind triumphed over all my wisdom; his darts were of greater force than all my reasonings, and with a sweet constraint he led me wherever he pleased. Heaven, amidst an abundance of blessings with which I was intoxicated, threw in a heavy affliction. I became a most signal example of its vengeance, and the more unhappy because, having deprived me of the means of accomplishing satisfaction, it left me to the fury of my criminal desires. I will tell you, my dear friend, the particulars of my story, and leave you to judge whether I deserved so severe a correction.

I had always an aversion for those light women whom 'tis a reproach to pursue; I was ambitious in my choice, and wished to find some obstacles, that I might surmount them with the greater glory and pleasure.

There was in Paris a young creature (ah, Philintus!) formed in a prodigality of nature to show mankind a finished composition; dear Héloïse, the reputed niece of one Fulbert, a canon. Her wit and her beauty would have stirred the dullest and most insensible heart, and her education was equally admirable. Héloïse was the mistress of the most polite arts. You may easily imagine that this did not a little help to captivate me; I saw her, I loved her, I resolved to make her love me. The thirst of glory cooled immediately in my heart, and all my passions were lost in this new one. I thought of nothing but Héloïse; everything brought her image to my mind. I was pensive and restless, and my passion was so violent as to admit of no restraint. I was always vain and presumptive; I flattered myself already with the most bewitching hopes. My reputation had spread itself everywhere, and could a virtuous lady resist a man who had confounded all the learned of the age? I was young—could she show an insensibility to those vows which my heart never formed for any but herself? My person was advantageous enough, and by my dress no one would have suspected me for a doctor; and dress, you know, is not a little engaging with women. Besides, I had wit enough to write a billet-doux, and hoped, if ever she permitted my absent self to entertain her, she would read with pleasure those breathings of my heart.

Filled with these notions I thought of nothing but the means to speak to her. Lovers either find or make all things easy. By the offices of common friends I gained the acquaintance of Fulbert; and can you believe it, Philintus, he allowed me the privilege of his table, and an apartment in his house?

I paid him, indeed, a considerable sum, for persons of his character do nothing without money. But what would I not have given! You, my friend, know what love is; imagine then what a pleasure it must have been to a heart so inflamed as mine to be always so near the dear object of desire! I would not have exchanged my happy condition for that of the greatest monarch upon earth. I saw Héloïse, I spoke to her—each action, each confused look told her the trouble of my soul. And she, on the other side, gave me ground to hope for everything from her generosity. Fulbert desired me to instruct her in philosophy; by this means I found opportunities of being in private with her, and yet I was surely of all men the most timorous in declaring my passion.

As I was with her one day alone, 'Charming Héloïse,' said I, blushing, 'if you know yourself you will not be surprised with the passion you have inspired me with. Uncommon as it is, I can express it but with the common terms—I love you, adorable Héloïse! Till now I thought philosophy made us masters of all our passions, and that it was a refuge from the storms in which weak mortals are tossed and shipwrecked; but you have destroyed my security and broken this philosophic courage. I have despised riches; honour and its pageantries could never wake a weak thought in me, beauty alone has stirred my soul; happy if she who raised this passion kindly receives this declaration; but if it is an offence?—'

'No,' replied Héloïse, 'she must be very ignorant of your merit who can be offended at your passion. But for my own repose I wish either that you had not made this declaration, or that I were at liberty not to suspect your sincerity.'

'Ah, divine Héloïse, said I, flinging myself at her feet, 'I swear by yourself—' I was going on to convince her of the truth of my passion, but heard a noise, and it was Fulbert: there was no avoiding it, I had to do violence to my desire and change the discourse to some other subject. After this I found frequent opportunities to free Héloïse from those suspicions which the general insincerity of men had raised in her; and she too much desired that what I said might be true not to believe it. Thus there was a most happy understanding between us. The same house, the same love, united our persons and our desires. How many soft moments did we pass together! We took all opportunities to express to each other our mutual affection, and were ingenious in contriving incidents which might give us a plausible occasion of meeting. Pyramus and Thisbe's discovery of the crack in the wall was but a slight representation of our love and its sagacity. In the dead of night, when Fulbert and his domestics were in a sound sleep, we improved the time proper with the sweets of love; not contenting ourselves, like those unfortunate lovers, with giving insipid kisses to a wall, we made use of all the moments of our charming interviews. In the place where we met we had no lions to fear, and the study of philosophy served us for a blind. But I was so far from making any advances in the sciences that I lost all my taste for them, and when I was obliged to go from the sight of my dear mistress to my philosophical exercises, it was with the utmost regret and melancholy. Love is incapable of being concealed; a word, a look, nay, silence, speaks it. My scholars discovered it first; they saw I had no longer that vivacity of thought to which all things are easy; I could now do nothing but write verses to soothe my passion. I quitted Aristotle and his dry maxims to practise the precepts of the more ingenious Ovid. No day passed in which I did not compose amorous verses; love was my inspiring Apollo. My songs were spread abroad and gained me frequent applause. Those who were in love as I was took a pride in learning them, and by luckily applying my thoughts and verses they obtained favours which perhaps they would not otherwise have gained. This gave our amours such an éclat that the lives of Héloïse and Abelard were the subject of all conversations.

The town talk at last reached Fulbert's ears; it was with great difficulty he gave credit to what he heard, for he loved his niece, and was prejudiced in my favour; but upon closer examination he began to be less credulous. He surprised us in one of our more tender conversations. How fatal sometimes are the consequences of curiosity! The anger of Fulbert seemed too moderate on this occasion, and I feared in the end some more heavy revenge. It is impossible to express the grief and regret which filled my soul when I was obliged to leave the Canon's house and my dear Héloïse. But this separation of our persons the more firmly united our minds; and the desperate condition we were reduced to made us capable of attempting anything.

My intrigues gave me but little shame, so lovingly did I regard the occasion; think what the gay young divinities said when Vulcan caught Mars and the Goddess of Beauty in his net, and impute it all to me. Fulbert surprised me with Héloïse, but what man that had a soul in him would not have borne any ignominy on the sane conditions? The next day I provided myself with a private lodging near the loved house, being resolved not to abandon my prey. I abode some time without appearing publicly. Ah! how long did those few days seem to me! When we fall from a state of happiness with what impatience do we bear our misfortunes!

It being impossible that I could live without seeing Héloïse, I endeavoured to engage her servant, whose name was Agaton, in my interest. She was brown, well-shaped, and a person superior to her rank; her features were regular and her eyes sparkling, fit to raise love in any man whose heart was not prepossessed by another passion. I met her alone and entreated her to have pity on a distressed lover. She answered she would undertake anything to serve me, but there was a reward. At these words I opened my purse and showed the shining metal which puts to sleep guards, forces a way through rocks, and softens the heart of the most obdurate fair.

'You are mistaken,' said she, smiling and shaking her head, 'you do not know me; could gold tempt me, a rich abbot takes his nightly station and sings under my window; he offers to send me to his abbey, which, he says, is situated in the most pleasant country in the world. A courtier offers me a considerable sum and assures me I need have no apprehension, for if our amours have consequences he will marry me to his gentleman and give him a handsome employment. To say nothing of a young officer who patrols about here every night and makes his attacks in all sorts of imaginable forms. It must be love only which could oblige him to follow me, for I have not, like your great ladies, any rings or jewels to tempt him. Yet, during all his siege of love, his feathers and his embroidered coat have not made any breach in my heart. I shall not quickly be brought to capitulate, I am too faithful to my first conqueror.'

She looked earnestly at me, and I said I did not understand.

'For a man of sense and gallantry,' she replied, 'you are slow of apprehension. I am in love with you, Abelard; I know you adore Héloïse, and I do not blame you, I desire only to enjoy the second place in your affections. I have a tender heart as well as my mistress; you may without difficulty make returns to my passion. Do not perplex yourself with scruples; a prudent man should love several at the sane time, then if one should fail he is not left unprovided.'

You can imagine, Philintus, how much I was surprised at these words: so entirely did I love Héloïse that, without reflecting whether Agaton spoke reasonably or not, I immediately left her. When I had gone a little way from her I looked back and saw her biting her nails in a rage of disappointment; this made me fear some fatal consequences. She hastened to Fulbert and told him the offer I had made her, but I suppose concealed the other part of the story. The Canon never forgave this affront; I afterwards perceived he was more deeply concerned for his niece than I had at first imagined. Let no lover hereafter follow my example, for a woman rejected is an outrageous creature. Agaton was at her window night and day on purpose to keep me away from her mistress, and so she gave her gallants every opportunity to display their abilities.

I was infinitely perplexed what course to take; at last I applied myself to Héloïse's singing-master. The shining metal, which had no effect on Agaton, charmed him: he was excellently qualified for conveying a billet with the greatest dexterity and secrecy. He delivered one of mine to Héloïse, who, according to my appointment, met me at the end of the garden, I having scaled the wall with a ladder of ropes. I confess to you all my failings, Philintus; how would my enemies Champeaux and Anselm have triumphed had they seen this redoubted philosopher in such a wretched condition. Well! I met my soul's joy—my Héloïse! I shall not transcribe our transports, they were not long, for the first news Héloïse acquainted me with plunged me into a thousand distractions. A floating Delos was to be sought for, where she might be safely delivered of a burden she began already to feel. Without losing much time in debating, I made her presently quit the Canon's house and at break of day depart for Brittany; where she, like another goddess, gave the world another Apollo, which my sister took care of.

This carrying off of Héloïse was sufficient revenge on Fulbert. It filled him with the deepest concern, and had like to have deprived him of the small share of wits which Heaven had allowed him. His sorrow and lamentation gave the censorious an occasion of suspecting him for something more than the uncle of Héloïse.

In short, I began to pity his misfortune, and to think this robbery which love had made me commit was a sort of treason. I endeavoured to appease his anger by a sincere confession of all that was past, and by hearty engagements to marry Héloïse secretly. He gave me his consent, and with many protestations and embraces confirmed our reconciliation. But what dependence can be made on the word of an ignorant devotee? He was only plotting a cruel revenge, as you will see by what follows.

I took a journey into Brittany in order to bring hack my dear Héloïse, whom I now considered my wife. When I had acquainted her with what had passed between the Canon and me I found she was of a contrary opinion to me. She urged all that was possible to divert me from marriage—that it was a bond always fatal to a philosopher; that the cries of children and the cares of a family were utterly inconsistent with the tranquillity and application which study require. She quoted to me all that was written on the subject by Theophrastus, Cicero, and, above all, insisted on the unfortunate Socrates, who quitted life with joy because by that means he left Xanthippe.

'Will it not be more agreeable to me,' said she, 'to see myself your mistress than your wife? And will not love have more power than marriage to keep our hearts firmly united? Pleasures tasted sparingly and with difficulty have always a higher relish, whilst everything that is easy and common grows stale and insipid.'

I was unmoved by all this reasoning, so Héloïse prevailed upon my sister to speak to me. Lucilla (for that was her name) therefore took me aside and said,—

'What do you intend, brother? Is it possible that Abelard should in earnest think of marrying Héloïse? She seems, indeed, to deserve a perpetual affection; beauty, youth and learning, all that can make a person valuable meet in her. You may adore all this if you please, but not to flatter you, what is beauty but a flower which may be blasted by the least fit of sickness? When those features with which you have been so captivated shall be sunk, and those graces lost, you will too late repent that you have entangled yourself in a chain from which death alone can free you. I shall see you reduced to the married man's only hope of survivorship. Do you think that learning makes Héloïse more amiable? I know she is not one of those affected females who are continually oppressing you with fine speeches, criticising looks, and deciding upon the merit of authors. When such a one is in the rush of her discourse, husband, friends and servants all fly before her. Héloïse has not this fault, yet 'tis troublesome not to be at liberty to use the least improper expression before a wife which you hear with pleasure from a mistress. But you say you are sure of the affection of Héloïse; I believe it; she has given you no ordinary proofs. But can you be sure marriage will not be the tomb of her love? The name of husband and master is always harsh, and Héloïse will not be the Phoenix you now think her. Will she not be a woman? Come, come, the head of a philosopher is less secure than those of other men!'

My sister grew warm in the argument, and was going on to give me a hundred more reasons of this kind, but I angrily interrupted her, telling her only that she did not know Héloïse.

12

A few days after we departed together from Brittany and came to Paris, where I completed my project. It was my intent my marriage should be kept secret, and therefore Héloïse retired among the nuns of Argenteuil.

I now thought Fulbert's anger disarmed; I lived in peace; but alas! our marriage proved but a weak defence against his revenge. Observe, Philintus, to what a barbarity he pursued it! He bribed my servants; an assassin came into my bedchamber by night, with a razor in his hand, and found me in a deep sleep. I suffered the most shameful punishment that the revenge of an enemy could invent; in short, without losing my life, I lost my manhood. So cruel an action escaped not justice, the villain suffered the same mutilation, poor comfort for so irretrievable an evil. I confess to you that shame more than any sincere penitence made me resolve to hide myself from the sight of men, yet could I not separate myself from my Héloïse. Jealousy took possession of my mind, and at the very expense of her happiness I decreed to disappoint all rivals. Before I put myself in a cloister I obliged her to take the habit and retire into the nunnery of Argenteuil. I remember somebody would have opposed her making such a cruel sacrifice of herself, but she answered in the words of Cornelia after the death of Pompey the Great,—

'O my loved lord, our fatal marriage draws
On thee this doom, and I the guilty cause!
Then whilst thou goest th' extremes of fate to prove,
I'll share that fate and expiate thus my love.'

Speaking these verses she marched up to the altar and took the veil with a constancy which I could not have expected in a woman who had so high a taste of pleasures which she might still enjoy. I blushed at my own weakness, and without deliberating a moment longer I buried myself in a cloister and resolved to vanquish a useless passion. I now reflected that God had chastised me thus grievously that He might save me from that destruction in which I had like to have been swallowed up. In order to avoid idleness, the unhappy incendiary of those criminal flames which had ruined me in the world, I endeavoured in my retirement to put those talents to a good use which I had before so much abused. I gave the novices rules of divinity agreeable to the holy Fathers and Councils. In the meanwhile the enemies that my new fame had raised up,—and especially Alberic and Lotulf, who, after the death of their masters Champeaux and Anselm, assumed the sovereignty of learning,—began to attack me. They loaded me with the falsest imputations, and, notwithstanding all my defence, I had the mortification to see my books condemned by a Council and burnt. This was a the cutting sorrow, and, believe me, Philintus, former calamity I suffered by the cruelty of Fulbert was nothing in comparison to this.

The affront I had newly received and the scandalous debaucheries of the monks obliged me to banish myself, and retire near to Nogent. I lived in a desert where I flattered myself I should avoid fame and be secure from the malice of my enemies. I was again deceived. The desire of being taught by me drew crowds of auditors even hither. Many left the towns and their houses, and came and lived in tents; for herbs, coarse fare and hard lodging, they abandoned the delicacies of a plentiful table and an easy life. I looked like the prophet in the wilderness attended by his disciples. My lectures were perfectly clear from all that had been condemned. Happy had it been if our solitude had been inaccessible to envy! With the considerable gratuities I received I built a chapel, and dedicated it to the Holy Ghost by the name of the Paraclete. The rage of my enemies now awakened again and forced me to quit this retreat. This I did without much difficulty, but first the Bishop of Troyes gave me leave to establish there a nunnery, and commit it to the care of my dear Héloïse. When I had settled her there, can you believe it, Philintus, I left her without taking leave.

I did not wander long without any settled habitation, for the Duke of Brittany, informed of my misfortunes, named me to the Abbey of St. Gildas, where I now am, and where I suffer every day fresh persecutions.

I live in a barbarous country, the language of which I don't understand; I have no conversation but with the rudest people. My walks are on the inaccessible shore of a sea which is always stormy. My monks are known only for their dissoluteness, and live without any rule or order. Could you see the abbey, Philintus, you would not recognise it for one: the doors and walls are without any ornament save the heads of wild boars and the feet of hinds, which are nailed up, and the hides of frightful animals. The cells are hung with the skins of deer; the monks have not so much as a bell to wake them, the cocks and dogs supply that defect. In short, they pass their time in hunting, and I would to God that were their greatest fault! Their pleasures do not terminate there, and I try in vain to recall them to their duty; they all combine against me, and I only expose myself to continual vexations and dangers. I imagine I see every moment a naked sword hang over my head. Sometimes they surround me and load me with infinite abuses; sometimes they abandon me, and I am left alone to my own tormenting thoughts. I make it my endeavour to merit by my sufferings and so appease an angry God. Sometimes I grieve for the loss of the house of the Paraclete and wish to see it again. Ah, Philintus! does not the love for Héloïse yet burn in my heart! I have not yet triumphed over that unhappy passion. In the midst of my retirement I sigh, I weep, I pine, I speak the dear name of Héloïse, and delight to hear the sound! I complain of the severity of Heaven; but oh! let us not deceive ourselves, I have not yet made a right use of grace. I am thoroughly wretched; I have not yet torn from my heart the deep roots which vice has planted in it, for if my conversion were sincere, how could I take pleasure in relating my past faults? Could I not more easily comfort myself in my afflictions; could I not turn to my advantage those words of God Himself—If they have persecuted Me they will also persecute you; if the world hate you, ye know that it hated Me also. Come, Philintus, let us make a strong effort, turn our misfortunes to our advantage, make them meritorious, or at least wipe out our offences: let us receive without murmuring what comes from the hand of God, and let us not oppose our will to His. Adieu; I give you advice which, could I myself follow, I should be happy.

Letter 2:

Héloïse to Abelard

T o her Lord, her Father, her Husband, her Brother; his Servant, his Child, his Wife, his Sister, and to express all that is humble, respectful and loving to her Abelard, Héloïse writes this.

A consolatory letter of yours to a friend happened some days since to fall into my hands; my knowledge of the writing and my love of the hand gave me the curiosity to open it. In justification of the liberty I took, I flattered myself I might claim a sovereign privilege over everything which came from you. Nor was I scrupulous to break through the rules of good breeding when I was to hear news of Abelard. But how dear did my curiosity cost me! What disturbance did it occasion, and how surprised I was to find the whole letter filled with a particular and melancholy account of our misfortunes! I met with my name a hundred times; I never saw it without fear, some heavy calamity always followed it. I saw yours too, equally unhappy. These mournful but dear remembrances put my heart into such violent motion that I thought it was too much to offer comfort to a friend for a few slight disgraces, but such extraordinary means as the representation of our sufferings and revolutions.

What reflections did I not make! I began to consider the whole afresh, and perceived myself pressed with the same weight of grief as when we first began to be miserable. Though length of time ought to have closed up my wounds, yet the seeing them described by your hand was sufficient to make them all open and bleed afresh. Nothing can ever blot from my memory what you have suffered in defence of your writings. I cannot help thinking of the rancorous malice of Alberic and Lotulf. A cruel Uncle and an injured Lover will always be present to my aching sight. I shall never forget what enemies your learning, and what envy your glory raised against you. I shall never forget your reputation, so justly acquired, torn to pieces and blasted by the inexorable cruelty of pseudo pretenders to science. Was not your treatise of Divinity condemned to be burnt? Were you not threatened with perpetual imprisonment? In vain you urged in your defence that your enemies imposed upon you opinions quite different from your meanings. In vain you condemned those opinions; all was of no effect towards your justification, 'twas resolved you should be a heretic! What did not those two false prophets accuse you of who declaimed so severely against you before the Council of Sens? What scandals were vented on occasion of the name of Paraclete given to your chapel! What a storm was

16

raised against you by the treacherous monks when you did them the honour to be called their brother! This history of our numerous misfortunes, related in so true and moving a manner, made my heart bleed within me my tears, which I could not refrain, have blotted half your letter; I wish they had effaced the whole, and that I had returned it to you in that condition; I should then have been satisfied with the little time I kept it; but it was demanded of me too soon.

I must confess I was much easier in my mind before I read your letter. Surely all the misfortunes of lovers are conveyed to them through the eyes: upon reading your letter I feel all mine renewed. I reproached myself for having been so long without venting my sorrows, when the rage of our unrelenting enemies still burns with the same fury. Since length of time, which disarms the strongest hatred, seems but to aggravate theirs; since it is decreed that your virtue shall be persecuted till it takes refuge in the grave—and even then, perhaps, your ashes will not be allowed to rest in peace!—let me always meditate on your calamities, let me publish them through all the world, if possible, to shame an age that has not known how to value you. I will spare no one since no one would interest himself to protect you, and your enemies are never weary of oppressing your innocence. Alas! my memory is perpetually filled with bitter remembrances of passed evils; and are there more to be feared still? Shall my Abelard never be mentioned without tears? Shall the dear name never be spoken but with sighs? Observe, I beseech you, to what a wretched condition you have reduced me; sad, afflicted, without any possible comfort unless it proceed from you. Be not then unkind, nor deny me, I beg of you, that little relief which you. Let me have a faithful account of all that concerns you; I would know everything, be it ever so unfortunate. Perhaps by mingling my sighs with yours I may make your sufferings less, for it is said that all sorrows divided are made lighter.

Tell me not by way of excuse you will spare me tears; the tears of women shut up in a melancholy place and devoted to penitence are not to be spared. And if you wait for an opportunity to write pleasant and agreeable things to us, you will delay writing too long. Prosperity seldom chooses the side of the virtuous, and fortune is so blind that in a crowd in which there is perhaps but one wise and brave man it is not to be expected that she should single him out. Write to me then immediately and wait not for miracles; they are too scarce, and we too much accustomed to misfortunes to expect a happy turn. I shall always have this, if you please, and this will always be agreeable to me, that when I receive any letter from you I shall know you still remember me. Seneca (with whose writings you made me acquainted), though he was a Stoic, seemed to be so very sensible to this kind of pleasure, that upon opening any letters from Lucilius he imagined he felt the same delight as when they conversed together.

I have made it an observation since our absence, that we are much fonder of the pictures of those we love when they are at a great distance than when they are near us. It seems to me as if the farther they are removed their pictures grow the more finished, and acquire a greater resemblance; or at least our imagination, which perpetually figures them to us by the desire we have of seeing them again, makes us think so. By a peculiar power love can make that seem life itself which, as soon as the loved object returns, is nothing but a little canvas and flat colour. I have your picture in my room; I never pass it without stopping to look at it; and yet when you are present with me I scarce ever cast my eyes on it. If a picture, which is but a mute representation of an object, can give such pleasure, what cannot letters inspire? They have souls; they can speak; they have in them all that force which expresses the transports of the heart; they have all the fire of our passions, they can raise them as much as if the persons themselves were present; they have all the tenderness and the delicacy of speech, and sometimes even a boldness of expression beyond it.

We may write to each other; so innocent a pleasure is not denied us. Let us not lose through negligence the only happiness which is left us, and the only one perhaps which the malice of our enemies can never ravish from us. I shall read that you are my husband and you shall see me sign myself your wife. In spite of all our misfortunes you may be what you please in your letter. Letters were first invented for consoling such solitary wretches as myself. Having lost the substantial pleasures of seeing and possessing you, I shall in some measure compensate this loss by the satisfaction I shall find in your writing. There I. shall read your most sacred thoughts; I shall carry them always about with me, I shall kiss them every moment; if you can be capable of any jealousy let it be for the fond caresses I shall bestow upon your letters, and envy only the happiness of those rivals. That writing may be no trouble to you, write always to me carelessly and without study; I had rather read the dictates of the heart than of the brain. I cannot live if you will not tell me that you still love me; but that language ought to be so natural to you, that I believe you cannot speak otherwise to me without violence to yourself. And since by this melancholy relation to your friend you have awakened all my sorrows, 'tis but reasonable you should allay them by some tokens of your unchanging love.

I do not however reproach you for the innocent artifice you made use of to comfort a person in affliction by comparing his misfortune to another far greater. Charity is ingenious in finding out such pious plans, and to be commended for using them. But do you owe nothing more to us than to that friend—be the friendship between you ever so intimate? We are called your Sisters; we call ourselves your children, and if it were possible to think of any expression which could signify a dearer relation, or a more affectionate regard and mutual obligation between us, we should use it. If we could be so ungrateful as not to speak our just acknowledgments to you, this church, these altars, these walls, would reproach our silence and speak for us. But without leaving it to that, it will always be a pleasure to me to say that you only are the founder of this house, 'tis wholly your work. You, by inhabiting here, have given fame and holiness to a place known before only for robberies and murders. You have in a literal sense made the den of thieves into a house of prayer. These cloisters owe nothing to public charities; our walls were not raised by the usuries of publicans, nor their foundations laid in base extortion. The God whom we serve sees nothing but innocent riches and harmless votaries whom . you have placed here. Whatever this young vineyard is, is owing only to you, and it is your part to employ your whole care to cultivate and improve it; this ought to be one of the principal affairs of your life. Though our holy renunciation, our vows and our manner of life seem to secure us from all temptation; though our walls and gates prohibit all approaches, yet it is the outside only, the bark of the tree, that is protected from injuries; the sap of the original corruption may imperceptibly spread within, even to the heart, and prove fatal to the most promising plantation, unless continual care be taken to cultivate and secure it. Virtue in us is grafted upon nature and the woman; the one is changeable, the other is weak. To plant the Lord's vineyard is a work of no little labour; but after it is planted it will require great application and diligence to dress it. The Apostle of the Gentiles, great labourer as he was, says he hath planted, Apollos hath watered, but it is God that gives the increase. Paul had planted the Gospel amongst the Corinthians, Apollos, his zealous disciple, continued to cultivate it by frequent exhortations; and the grace of God, which their constant prayers implored for that church, made the work of both be fruitful.

This ought to be an example for your conduct towards us. I know you are not slothful, yet your labours are not directed towards us; your cares are wasted upon a set of men whose thoughts are only earthly, and you refuse to reach out your hand to support those who are weak and staggering in their way to heaven, and who with all their endeavours can scarcely prevent themselves from falling. You fling the pearls of the Gospel before swine when you speak to those who are filled with the good things of this world and nourished with the fatness of the earth; and you neglect the innocent sheep, who, tender as they are, would yet follow you over deserts and mountains. Why are such pains thrown away upon the ungrateful, while not a thought is bestowed upon your children, whose souls would be filled with a sense of your goodness? But why should I entreat you in the name of your children? Is it possible I should fear obtaining anything of you when I ask it in my own name? And must I use any other prayers than my own in order to prevail upon you? The St. Austins, Tertullians and Jeromes have written to the Eudoxias, Paulas and Melanias; and can you read those names, though of saints, and not remember mine? Can it be criminal for you to imitate St. Jerome and discourse with me concerning the Scriptures; or Tertullian and preach mortification; or St. Austin and explain to me the nature of grace? Why should I alone not reap the advantage of your learning? When you write to me you will write to your wife; marriage has made such a correspondence lawful, and since you can without the least scandal satisfy me, why will you not? I am not only engaged by my vows, but I have the fear of my Uncle before me. There is nothing, then, that you need dread; you need not fly to conquer. You may see me, hear my sighs, and be a witness of all my sorrows without incurring any danger, since you can only relieve me with tears and words. If I have put myself into a cloister with reason, persuade me to stay in it with devotion. You have been the occasion of all my misfortunes, you therefore must be the instrument of all my comfort.

You cannot but remember (for lovers cannot forget) with what pleasure I have passed whole days in hearing your discourse. How when you were absent I shut myself from everyone to write to you; how uneasy I was till my letter had come to your hands; what artful management it required to engage messengers. This detail perhaps surprises you, and you are in pain for what may follow. But I am no longer ashamed that my passion had no bounds for you, for I have done more than all this. I have hated myself that I might love you; I came hither to ruin myself in a perpetual imprisonment that I might make you live quietly and at ease. Nothing but virtue, joined to a love perfectly disengaged from the senses, could have produced such effects. Vice never inspires anything like this, it is too much enslaved to the body. When we love pleasures we love the living and not the dead. We leave off burning with desire for those who can no longer burn for us. This was my cruel Uncle's notion; he measured my virtue by the frailty of my sex, and thought it was the man and not the person I loved. But he has been guilty to no purpose. I love you more than ever; and so revenge myself on him. I will still love you with all the tenderness of my soul till the last moment of my life. If, formerly, my affection for you was not so pure, if in those days both mind and body loved you, I often told you even then that I was more pleased with possessing your heart than with any other happiness, and the man was the thing I least valued in you.

You cannot but be entirely persuaded of this by the extreme unwillingness I showed to marry you, though I knew that the name of wife was honourable in the world and holy in religion; yet the name of your mistress had greater charms because it was more free. The bonds of matrimony, however honourable, still bear with them a necessary engagement, and I was very unwilling to be necessitated to love always a man who would perhaps not always love me. I despised the name of wife that I might live happy with that of mistress; and I find by your letter to your friend you have not forgot that delicacy of passion which loved you always with the utmost tenderness—and yet wished to love you more! You have very justly observed in your letter that I esteemed those public engagements insipid which form alliances only to be dissolved by death, and which put life and love under the same unhappy necessity. But

20

you have not added how often I have protested that it was infinitely prefer-able to me to live with Abelard as his mistress than with any other as Empress of the World. I was more happy in obeying you than I should have been as lawful spouse of the King of the Earth. Riches and pomp are not the charm of love. True tenderness makes us separate the lover from all that is external to him, and setting aside his position, fortune or employments, consider him merely as himself.

It is not love, but the desire of riches and position which makes a woman run into the embraces of an indolent husband. Ambition, and not affection, forms such marriages. I believe indeed they may be followed with some hon-ours and advantages, but I can never think that this is the way to experience the pleasures of affectionate union, nor to feel those subtle and charming joys when hearts long parted are at last united. These martyrs of marriage pine always for larger fortunes which they think they have missed. The wife sees . husbands richer than her own, and the husband wives better portioned than his. Their mercenary vows occasion regret, and regret produces hatred. Soon they part—or else desire to. This restless and tormenting passion for gold punishes them for aiming at other advantages by love than love itself.

If there is anything that may properly be called happiness here below, I am persuaded it is the union of two persons who love each other with perfect liberty, who are united by a secret inclination, and satisfied with each other's merits. Their hearts are full and leave no vacancy for any other passion; they enjoy perpetual tranquillity because they enjoy content.

If I could believe you as truly persuaded of my merit as I am of yours, I might say there has been a time when we were such a pair. Alas! how was it possible I should not be certain of your mind? If I could ever have doubted it, the universal esteem would have made me decide in your favour. What country, what city, has not desired your presence? Could you ever retire but you drew the eyes and hearts of all after you? Did not everyone rejoice in having seen you? Even women, breaking through the laws of decorum which custom had imposed upon them, showed they felt more for you than mere esteem. I have known some who have been profuse in their husbands' praises who have yet envied me my happiness. But what could resist you? Your reputation, which so much attracts the vanity of our sex, your air, your manner, that light in your eyes which expresses the vivacity of your mind, your conversation so easy and elegant that it gave everything you said an agreeable turn; in short, everything spoke for you! Very different from those mere scholars who with all their learning have not the capacity to keep up an ordinary conversation, and who with all their wit cannot win a woman who has much less share of brains than themselves.

With what ease did you compose verses! And yet those ingenious trifles, which were but a recreation to you, are still the entertainment and delight of persons of the best taste. The smallest song, the least sketch of anything you made for me, had a thousand beauties capable of making it last as long as there are lovers in the world. Thus those songs will be sung in honour of other women which you designed only for me, and those tender and natural expressions which spoke your love will help others to explain their passion with much more advantage than they themselves are capable of.

What rivalries did your gallantries of this kind occasion me! How many ladies lay claim to them? 'Twas a tribute their self-love paid to their beauty. How many have I seen with sighs declare their passion for you when, after some common visit you had made them, they chanced to be complimented for the Sylvia of your poems. Others in despair and envy have reproached me that I had no charms but what your wit bestowed on me, nor in anything the advantage over them but in being beloved by you. Can you believe me if I tell you, that notwithstanding my sex, I thought myself peculiarly happy in having a lover to whom I was obliged for my charms; and took a secret pleasure in being admired by a man who, when he pleased, could raise his mistress to the character of a goddess. Pleased with your glory only, I read with delight all those praises you offered me, and without reflecting how little I deserved, I believed myself such as you described, that I might be more certain that I pleased you.

But oh! where is that happy time? I now lament my lover, and of all my joys have nothing but the painful memory that they are past. Now learn, all you my rivals who once viewed my happiness with jealous eyes, that he you once envied me can never more be mine. I loved him; my love was his crime and the cause of his punishment. My beauty once charmed him; pleased with each other we passed our brightest days in tranquillity and happiness. If that were a crime, 'tis a crime I am yet fond of, and I have no other regret save that against my will I must now be innocent. But what do I say? My misfortune was to have cruel relatives whose malice destroyed the calm we enjoyed; had they been reasonable I had now been happy in the enjoyment of my dear husband. Oh! how cruel were they when their blind fury urged a villain to surprise you in your sleep! Where was I—where was your Héloïse then? What joy should I have had in defending my lover; I would have guarded you from violence at the expense of my life. Oh! whither does this excess of passion hurry me? Here love is shocked and modesty deprives me of words.

But tell me whence proceeds your neglect of me since my being professed? You know nothing moved me to it but your disgrace, nor did I give my consent, but yours. Let me hear what is the occasion of your coldness, or give me leave to tell you now my opinion. Was it not the sole thought of pleasure which engaged you to me? And has not my tenderness, by leaving you nothing to wish for, extinguished your desires? Wretched Héloïse! you could please when you wished to avoid it; you merited incense when you could remove to a distance the hand that offered it: but since your heart has been softened and has yielded, since you have devoted and sacrificed yourself, you are deserted and forgotten! I am convinced by a sad experience that it is natural to avoid those to whom we have been too much obliged, and that uncommon generosity causes neglect rather than gratitude. My heart surrendered too soon to gain the esteem of the conqueror; you took it without difficulty and throw it aside with ease. But ungrateful as you are I am no consenting party to this, and though I ought not to retain a wish of my own, yet I still preserve secretly the desire to be loved by you. When I pronounced my sad vow I then had about me your last letters in which you protested your whole being wholly mine, and would never live but to love me. It is to you therefore I have offered myself; you had my heart and I had yours; do not demand anything back. You must bear with my passion as a thing which of right belongs to you, and from which you can be no ways disengaged.

Alas! what folly it is to talk in this way! I see nothing here but marks of the Deity, and I speak of nothing but man! You have been the cruel occasion of this by your conduct, Unfaithful One! Ought you at once to break off loving me! Why did you not deceive me for a while rather than immediately abandon me? If you had given me at least some faint signs of a dying passion I would have favoured the deception. But in vain do I flatter myself that you could be constant; you have left no vestige of an excuse for you. I am earnestly desirous to see you, but if that be impossible I will content myself with a few lines from your hand. Is it so hard for one who loves to write? I ask for none of your letters filled with learning and writ for your reputation; all I desire is such letters as the heart dictates, and which the hand cannot transcribe fast enough. How did I deceive myself with hopes that you would be wholly mine when I took the veil, and engage myself to live for ever under your laws? For in being professed I vowed no more than to be yours only, and I forced myself voluntarily to a confinement which you desired for me. Death only then can make me leave the cloister where you have placed me; and then my ashes shall rest here and wait for yours in order to show to the very last my obedience and devotion to you.

Why should I conceal from you the secret of my call? You know it was neither zeal nor devotion that brought me here. Your conscience is too faithful a witness to permit you to disown it. Yet here I am, and here I will remain; to this place an unfortunate love and a cruel relation have condemned me. But if you do not continue your concern for me, if I lose your affection, what have I gained by my imprisonment? What recompense can I hope for? The unhappy consequences of our love and your disgrace have made me put on the habit of chastity, but I am not penitent of the past. Thus I strive and labour in vain. Among those who are wedded to God I am wedded to a man; among the heroic supporters of the Cross I am the slave of a human desire;

at the head of a religious community I am devoted to Abelard alone. What a monster am I! Enlighten me, O Lord, for I know not if my despair or Thy grace draws these words from me! I am, I confess, a sinner, but one who, far from weeping for her sins, weeps only for her lover; far from abhorring her crimes, longs only to add to them; and who, with a weakness unbecoming my state, please myself continually with the remembrance of past delights when it is impossible to renew them.

Good God! What is all this? I reproach myself for my own faults, I accuse you for yours, and to what purpose? Veiled as I am, behold in what a disorder you have plunged me! How difficult it is to fight for duty against inclination. I know what obligations this veil lays upon me, but I feel more strongly what power an old passion has over my heart. I am conquered by my feelings; love troubles my mind and disorders my will. Sometimes I am swayed by the sentiment of piety which arises within me, and then the next moment I yield up my imagination to all that is amorous and tender. I tell you to-day what I would not have said to you yesterday. I had resolved to love you no more; I considered I had made a vow, taken a veil, and am as it were dead and buried, yet there rises unexpectedly from the bottom of my heart a passion which triumphs over all these thoughts, and darkens alike my reason and my religion. You reign in such inward retreats of my soul that I know not where to attack you; when I endeavour to break those chains by which I am bound to you I only deceive myself, and all my efforts but serve to bind them faster. Oh, for pity's sake help a wretch to renounce her desires—her self—and if possible even to renounce you! If you are a lover—a father, help a mistress, comfort a child! These tender names must surely move you; yield either to pity or to love. If you gratify my request I shall continue a religious, and without longer profaning my calling. I am ready to humble myself with you to the wonderful goodness of God, Who does all things for our sanctification, Who by His grace purifies all that is vicious and corrupt, and by the great riches of His mercy draws us against our wishes, and by degrees opens our eyes to behold His bounty which at first we could not perceive.

I thought to end my letter here, but now I am complaining against you I must unload my heart and tell you all its jealousies and reproaches. Indeed I thought it somewhat bard that when we had both engaged to consecrate ourselves to Heaven you should insist upon my doing it first. 'Does Abelard then,' said I, 'suspect that, like Lot's wife, I shall look back?' If my youth and sex might give occasion of fear that I should return to the world, could not my behaviour, my fidelity, and this heart which you ought to know, banish such ungenerous apprehensions? This distrust hurt me; I said to myself, 'There was a time when he could rely upon my bare word, and does he now want vows to secure himself to me? What occasion have I given him in the whole course of my life to admit the least suspicion? I could meet him at all his assignations, and would I decline to follow him to the Seats of Holiness? I, who have not refused to be the victim of pleasure in order to gratify him, can he think I would refuse to be a sacrifice of honour when he desired it?' Has vice such charms to refined natures, that when once we have drunk of the cup of sinners it is with such difficulty we accept the chalice of saints? Or did you believe yourself to be more competent to teach vice than virtue,

The Purity of her loveor me more ready to learn the first than the latter? No; this suspicion would be injurious to us both: Virtue is too beautiful not to be embraced when you reveal her charms, and Vice too hideous not to be abhorred when you display her deformities. Nay, when you please, anything seems lovely to me, and nothing is ugly when you are by. I am only weak when I am alone and unsupported by you, and therefore it depends on you alone to make me such as you desire. I wish to Heaven you had not such a power over me! If you had any occasion to fear you would be less negligent. But what is there for you to fear? I have done too much, and now have nothing more to do but to triumph over your ingratitude. When we lived happily together you might have doubted whether pleasure or affection united me more to you, but the place from whence I write to you must surely have dissolved all doubt. Even here I love you as much as ever I did in the world. If I had loved pleasures could I not have found means to gratify myself? I was not more than twenty-two years old, and there were other men left though I was deprived of Abelard. And yet I buried myself alive in a nunnery, and triumphed over life at an age capable of enjoying it to its full latitude. It is to you I sacrifice these remains of a transitory beauty, these widowed nights and tedious days; and since you cannot possess them I take them from you to offer them to Heaven, and so make, alas! but a secondary oblation of my heart, my days, my life!

I am sensible I have dwelt too long on this subject; I ought to speak less to you of your misfortunes and of my sufferings. We tarnish the lustre of our most beautiful actions when we applaud them ourselves. This is true, and yet there is a time when we may with decency commend ourselves; when we have to do with those whom base ingratitude has stupefied we cannot too much praise our own actions. Now if you were this sort of creature this would be a home reflection on you. Irresolute as I am I still love you, and yet I must hope for nothing. I have renounced life, and stript myself of everything, but I find I neither have nor can renounce my Abelard. Though I have lost my lover I still preserve my love. O vows! O convent! I have not lost my humanity under your inexorable discipline! You have not turned me to marble by changing my habit; my heart is not hardened by my imprisonment; I am still sensible to what has touched me, though, alas! I ought not to be! Without offending your commands permit a lover to exhort me to live in obedience to your rigorous rules. Your yoke will be lighter if that hand support me under it; your exercises will be pleasant if he show me their advantage. Retirement and solitude will no longer seem terrible if I may know that I still have a place in his memory. A heart which has loved as mine cannot soon be indifferent. We fluctuate long between love and hatred before we can arrive at tranquillity, and we always flatter ourselves with some forlorn hope that we shall not be utterly forgotten.

Yes, Abelard, I conjure you by the chains I bear here to ease the weight of them, and make them as agreeable as I would they were to me.

Teach me the maxims of Divine Love; since you have forsaken me I would glory in being wedded to Heaven. My heart adores that title and disdains any other; tell me how this Divine Love is nourished, how it works, how it purifies. When we were tossed on the ocean of the world we could hear of nothing but your verses, which published everywhere our joys and pleasures. Now we are in the haven of grace is it not fit you should discourse to me of this new happiness, and teach me everything that might heighten or improve it? Show me the same complaisance in my present condition as you did when we were in the world. Without changing the ardour of our affections let us change their objects; let us leave our songs and sing hymns; let us lift up our hearts to God and have no transports but for His glory!

I expect this from you as a thing you cannot refuse me. God has a peculiar right over the hearts of great men He has created. When He pleases to touch them He ravishes them, and lets them not speak nor breathe but for His glory. Till that moment of grace arrives, O think of me—do not forget me—remember my love and fidelity and constancy: love me as your mistress, cherish me as your child, your sister, your wife! Remember I still love you, and yet strive to avoid loving you. What a terrible saying is this! I shake with horror, and my heart revolts against what I say. I shall blot all my paper with tears. I end my long letter wishing you, if you desire it (would to Heaven I could!), for ever adieu!

Letter 3:

Abelard to Héloïse

Could I have imagined that a letter not written to yourself would fall into your hands, I had been more cautious not to have inserted anything in it which might awaken the memory of our past misfortunes. I described with boldness the series of my disgraces to a friend, in order to make him less sensible to a loss he had sustained. If by this well-meaning device I have disturbed you, I purpose now to dry up those tears which the sad description occasioned you to shed; I intend to mix my grief with yours, and pour out my heart before you: in short, to lay open before your eyes all my trouble, and the secret of my soul, which my vanity has hitherto made me conceal from the rest of the world, and which you now force from me, in spite of my resolutions to the contrary.

It is true, that in a sense of the afflictions which have befallen us, and observing that no change of our condition could be expected; that those prosperous days which had seduced us were now past, and there remained nothing but to erase from our minds, by painful endeavours, all marks and remembrances of them. I had wished to find in philosophy and religion a remedy for my disgrace; I searched out an asylum to secure me from love. I was come to the sad experiment

The greater the silence, the louder speaks loveof making vows to harden my heart. But what have I gained by this? If my passion has been put under a restraint my thoughts yet run free. I promise myself that I will forget you, and yet cannot think of it without loving you. My love is not at all lessened by those reflections I make in order to free myself. The silence I am surrounded by makes me more sensible to its impressions, and while I am unemployed with any other things, this makes itself the business of my whole vacation. Till after a multitude of useless endeavours I begin to persuade myself that it is a superfluous trouble to strive to free myself; and that it is sufficient wisdom to conceal from all but you how confused and weak I am.

I remove to a distance from your person with an intention of avoiding you as an enemy; and yet I incessantly seek for you in my mind; I recall your image in my memory, and in different disquietudes I betray and contradict myself. I hate you! I love you! Shame presses me on all sides. I am at this moment afraid I should seem more indifferent than you fare, and yet I am ashamed to discover my trouble. How weak are we in ourselves if we do not support ourselves on the Cross of Christ. Shall we have so little courage, and shall that uncertainty of serving two masters which afflicts your heart affect mine too? You see the confusion I am in, how I blame myself and how I suffer. Religion commands me to pursue virtue since I have nothing to hope for from love. But love still preserves its dominion over my fancies and entertains itself with past pleasures. Memory supplies the place of a mistress. Piety and duty are not always the fruits of retirement; even in deserts, when the dew of heaven falls not on us, we love what we ought no longer to love. The passions, stirred up by solitude, fill these regions of death and silence; it is very seldom that what ought to be is truly followed here and that God only is loved and served. Had I known this before I had instructed you better. You call me your master; it is true you were entrusted to my care. I saw you, I was earnest to teach you vain sciences; it cost you your innocence and me my liberty. Your Uncle, who was fond of you, became my enemy and revenged himself on me. If now having lost the power of satisfying my passion I had also lost that of loving you, I should have some consolation. My enemies would have given me that tranquillity which Origen purchased with a crime. How miserable am I! I find myself much more guilty in my thoughts of you, even amidst my tears, than in possessing you when I was in full liberty. I continually think of you; I continually call to mind your tenderness. In this condition, O Lord! if I run to prostrate myself before your altar, if I beseech you to pity me, why does not the pure flame of the Spirit consume the sacrifice that is offered? Cannot this habit of penitence which I wear interest Heaven to treat me more favourably? But Heaven is still inexorable because my passion still lives in me; the fire is only covered over with deceitful ashes, and cannot be extinguished but by extraordinary grace. We deceive men, but nothing is hid from God.

You tell me that it is for me you live under that veil which covers you; why do you profane your vocation with such words? Why provoke a jealous God with a blasphemy? I hoped after our separation you would have changed your sentiments; I hoped too that God would have delivered me from the tumult of my senses. We commonly die to the affections of those we see no more, and they to ours; absence is the tomb of love. But to me absence is an unquiet remembrance of what I once loved which continually torments me. I flattered myself that when I should see you no more you would rest in my memory without troubling my mind; that Brittany and the sea would suggest other thoughts; that my fasts and studies would by degrees delete you from my heart. But in spite of severe fasts and redoubled studies, in spite of the distance of three hundred miles which separates us, your image, as you describe yourself in your veil, appears to me and confounds all my resolutions.

What means have I not used! I have armed my hands against myself; I have exhausted my strength in constant exercises; I comment upon St. Paul; I contend with Aristotle: in short, I do all I used to do before I loved you, but

28

all in vain; nothing can be successful that opposes you. Oh! do not add to my miseries by your constancy; forget, if you can, your favours and that right which they claim over me; allow me to be indifferent. I envy their happiness who have never loved; how quiet and easy are they! But the tide of pleasure has always a reflux of bitterness; I am but too much convinced now of this: but though I am no longer deceived by love, I am not cured. While my reason condemns it my heart declares for it. I am deplorable that I have not the ability to free myself from a passion which so many circumstances, this place, my person and my disgraces tend to destroy; I yield without considering that a resistance would wipe out my past offences, and procure me in their stead both merit and repose. Why use your eloquence to reproach me for my flight and for my silence? Spare the recital of our assignations and your constant exactness to them; without calling up such disturbing thoughts I have enough to suffer. What great advantages would. philosophy give us over other men, if by studying it we could learn to govern our passions? What efforts, what relapses, what agitations do we undergo! And how long are we lost in this confusion, unable to exert our reason, to possess our souls, or to rule our affections?

What a troublesome employment is love! And how valuable is virtue even upon consideration of our own ease! Recollect your extravagancies of passion, guess at my distractions; number up our cares, our griefs; throw these things out of the account and let love have all the remaining tenderness and pleasure. How little is that! And yet for such shadows of enjoyments which at first appeared to us are we so weak our whole lives that we cannot now help writing to each other, covered as we are with sackcloth and ashes. How much happier should we be if by our humiliation and tears we could make our repentance sure. The love of pleasure is not eradicated out of the soul save by extraordinary efforts; it has an advocate in our breasts that we find it difficult to condemn it ourselves. What abhorrence can I be said to have of my sins if the objects of them are always amiable to me? How can I separate from the person I love the passion I should detest? Will the tears I shed be sufficient to render it odious to me? I know not how it happens, there is always a pleasure in weeping for a beloved object. It is difficult in our sorrow to distinguish penitence from love. The memory of the crime and the memory of the object which has charmed us are too nearly related to be immediately separated. And the love of God in its beginning does not wholly annihilate the love of the creature.

But what excuses could I not find in you if the crime were excusable? Unprofitable honour, troublesome riches, could never tempt me: but those charms, that beauty, that air, which I. yet behold at this instant, have occasioned my fall. Your looks were the beginning of my guilt; your eyes, your discourse, pierced my heart; and in spite of that ambition and glory which tried to make a defence, love was soon the master. God, in order to punish me, forsook me. You are no longer of the world; you have renounced it: I am a religious devoted to solitude; shall we not take advantage of our condition? Would you destroy my piety in its infant state? Would you have me forsake the abbey into which I am but newly entered? Must I renounce my vows? I have made them in the presence of God; whither shall I fly from His wrath should I violate them? Suffer me to seek ease in my duty: though difficult it is to procure it. I pass whole days and nights alone in this cloister without closing my eyes. My love burns fiercer amidst the happy indifference of those who surround me, and my heart is alike pierced with your sorrows and my own. Oh, what a loss have I sustained when I consider your constancy! What pleasures have I missed enjoying! I ought not to confess this weakness to you; I am sensible I commit a fault. If I could show more firmness of mind I might provoke your resentment against me and your anger might work that effect in you which your virtue could not. If in the world I published my weakness in love-songs and verses, ought not the dark cells of this house at least to conceal that same weakness under an appearance of piety? Alas! I am still the same! Or if I avoid the evil, I cannot do the good. Duty, reason and decency, which upon other occasions have some power over me, are here useless. The Gospel is a language I do not understand when it opposes my passion. Those vows I have taken before the altar are feeble when opposed to thoughts of you. Amidst so many voices which bid me do my duty, I hear and obey nothing but the secret cry of a desperate passion. Void of all relish for virtue, without concern for my condition or any application to my studies, I am continually present by my imagination where I ought not to be, and I find I have no power to correct myself. I feel a perpetual strife between inclination and duty. I find myself a distracted lover, unquiet in the midst of silence, and restless in the midst of peace. How shameful is such a condition!

Regard me no more, I entreat you, as a founder or any great personage; your praises ill agree with my many weaknesses. I am a miserable sinner, prostrate before my Judge, and with my face pressed to the earth I mix my tears with the earth. Can you see me in this posture and solicit me to love you? Come, if you think fit, and in your holy habit thrust yourself between my God and me, and be a wall of separation. Come and force from me those sighs and thoughts and vows I owe to Him alone. Assist the evil spirits and be the instrument of their malice. What cannot you induce a heart to do whose weakness you so perfectly know? Nay, withdraw yourself and contribute to my salvation. Suffer me to avoid destruction, I entreat you by our former tender affection and by our now common misfortune. It will always to show none; I here release you from all your oaths and engagements. Be God's wholly, to whom you are appropriated; I will never oppose so pious a design. How happy shall I be if I thus lose you! Then shall I indeed be a religious and you a perfect example of an abbess.

Make yourself amends by so glorious a choice; make your virtue a spectacle worthy of men and angels. Be humble among your children, assiduous in your choir, exact in your discipline, diligent in your reading; make even your recreations useful. Have you purchased your vocation at so light a rate that you should not turn it to the best advantage? Since you have permitted yourself to be abused by false doctrine and criminal instruction, resist not those good counsels which grace and religion inspire me with. I will confess to you I have thought myself hitherto an abler master to instil vice than to teach virtue. My false eloquence has only set off false good. My heart, drunk with voluptuousness, could only suggest terms proper and moving to recommend that. The cup of sinners overflows with so enchanting a 'sweetness, and we are naturally so much inclined to taste it, that it needs only to be offered to us. On the other hand the chalice of saints is filled with a bitter draught and nature starts from it. And yet you reproach me with cowardice for giving it to you first. I willingly submit to these accusations. I cannot enough admire the readiness you showed to accept the religious habit; bear therefore with courage the Cross you so resolutely took up. Drink of the chalice of saints, even to the bottom, without turning your eyes with uncertainty upon me; let me remove far from you and obey the Apostle who hath said 'Fly!'.

You entreat me to return under a pretence of devotion. Your earnestness in this point creates a suspicion in me and makes me doubtful how to answer you. Should I commit an error here my words would blush, if I may say so, after the history of our misfortunes. The Church is jealous of its honour, and commands that her children should be induced to the practice of virtue by virtuous means. When we approach God in a blameless manner then we may with boldness invite others to Him. But to forget Héloïse, to see her no more, is what Heaven demands of Abelard; and to expect nothing from Abelard, to I forget him even as an idea, is what Heaven enjoins yon Héloïse. To forget, in the case of love, is the most necessary penance, and the most difficult. It is easy to recount our faults; how many, through indiscretion, have made themselves a second pleasure of this instead of confessing them with humility. The only way to return to God is by neglecting the creature we have adored, and adoring the God whom we have neglected. This may appear harsh, but it must be done if we would be saved.

To make it more easy consider why I pressed you to your vow before I took mine; and pardon my sincerity and the design I have of meriting your neglect and hatred if I conceal nothing from you. When I saw myself oppressed by my misfortune I was furiously jealous, and regarded all men as my rivals. Love has more of distrust than assurance. I was apprehensive of many things because of my many defects, and being tormented with fear because of my own example I imagined your heart so accustomed to love that it could not be long without entering on a new engagement. Jealousy can easily believe the most terrible things. I was desirous to make it impossible for me to doubt you. I was very urgent to persuade you that propriety demanded your withdrawal from the eyes of the world; that modesty and our friendship required it; and that your own safety obliged it. After such a revenge taken on me you could expect to be secure nowhere but in a convent.

I will do you justice, you were very easily persuaded. My jealousy secretly rejoiced in your innocent compliance; and yet, triumphant as I was, I yielded you up to God with an unwilling heart.

I still kept my gift as much as was possible, and only parted with it in order to keep it out of the power of other men. I did not persuade you to religion out of any regard to your happiness, but condemned you to it like an enemy who destroys what he cannot carry off. And yet you heard my discourses with kindness, you sometimes interrupted me with tears, and pressed me to acquaint you with those convents I held in the highest esteem. What a comfort I felt in seeing you shut up. I was now at ease and took a satisfaction in considering that you continued no longer in the world after my disgrace, and that you would return to it no more.

But still I was doubtful. I imagined women were incapable of steadfast resolutions unless they were forced by the necessity of vows. I wanted those vows, and Heaven itself for your security, that I might no longer distrust you. Ye holy mansions and impenetrable retreats! from what innumerable apprehensions have ye freed me? Religion and piety keep a strict guard round your grates and walls. What a haven of rest this is to a jealous mind! And with what impatience did I endeavour after it! I went every day trembling to exhort you to this sacrifice; I admired, without daring to mention it then, a brightness in your beauty which I had never observed before. Whether it was the bloom of a rising virtue, or an anticipation of the great loss I was to suffer, I was not curious in examining the cause, but only hastened your being professed. I engaged your prioress in my guilt by a criminal bribe with which I purchased the right of burying you. The professed were alike bribed and concealed from you, at my directions, all their scruples and disgusts. I omitted nothing, either little or great; and if you had escaped my snares I myself would not have retired; I was resolved to follow you everywhere. The shadow of myself would always have pursued your steps and continually have occasioned either your confusion or your fear, which would have been a sensible gratification to me.

But, thanks to Heaven, you resolved to take the vows. I accompanied you to the foot of the altar, and while you stretched out your hand to touch the sacred cloth I heard you distinctly pronounce those fatal words that for ever separated you from man. Till then I thought your youth and beauty would foil my design and force your return to the world. Might not a small temptation have changed you? Is it possible to renounce oneself entirely at the age of two-and-twenty? At an age which claims the utmost liberty could you think the world no longer worth your regard? How much did I wrong you, and what weakness did I impute to you? You were in my imagination both light and inconstant. Would not a woman at the noise of the flames and the fall of Sodom involuntarily look back in pity on some person? I watched your eyes, your every movement, your air; I trembled at everything. You may call such self-interested conduct treachery, perfidy, murder. A love so like to hatred should provoke the utmost contempt and anger.

It is fit you should know that the very moment when I was convinced of your being entirely devoted to me, when I saw you were infinitely worthy of all my love, I imagined I could love you no more. I thought it time to leave off giving you marks of my affection, and I considered that by your Holy Espousals you were now the peculiar care of Heaven, and no longer a charge on me as my wife. My jealousy seemed to be extinguished. When God only is our rival we have nothing to fear; and being in greater tranquillity than ever before I even dared to pray to Him to take you away from my eyes. But it was not a time to make rash prayers, and my faith did not warrant them being heard. Necessity and despair were at the root of my proceedings, and thus I offered an insult to Heaven rather than a sacrifice. God rejected my offering and my prayer, and continued my punishment by suffering me to continue my love. Thus I bear alike the guilt of your vows and of the passion that preceded them, and must be tormented all the days of my life.

If God spoke to your heart as to that of a religious whose innocence had first asked him for favours, I should have matter of comfort; but to see both of us the victims of a guilty love, to see this love insult us in our very habits and spoil our devotions, fills me with horror and trembling. Is this a state of reprobation? Or are these the consequences of a long drunkenness in profane love? We cannot say love is a poison and a drunkenness till we are illuminated by Grace; in the meantime it is an evil we doat on. When we are under such a mistake, the knowledge of our misery is the first step towards amendment.

Who does not know that 'tis for the glory of God to find no other reason in man for His mercy than man's very weakness? When He has shown us this weakness and we have bewailed it, He is ready to put forth His Omnipotence and assist us. Let us say for our comfort that what we suffer is one of those terrible temptations which have sometimes disturbed the vocations of the most holy.

God can grant His presence to men in order to soften their calamities whenever He shall think fit. It was His pleasure when you took the veil to draw you to Him by His grace. I saw your eyes, when you spoke your last farewell, fixed upon the Cross. It was more than six months before you wrote me a letter, nor during all that time did I receive a message from you. I admired this silence, which I durst not blame, but could not imitate. I wrote to you, and you returned me no answer: your heart was then shut, but this garden of the spouse is now opened; He is withdrawn from it and has left you alone. By removing from you He has made trial of you; call Him back and strive to regain Him. We must have the assistance of God, that we may break our chains; we are too deeply in love to free ourselves. Our follies have penetrated into the sacred places; our amours have been a scandal to the whole kingdom. They are read and admired; love which produced them has caused them to be described. We shall be a consolation to the failings of youth for ever; those who offend after us will think themselves less guilty. We are criminals whose repentance is late; oh, let it be sincere! Let us repair as far as is possible the evils we have done, and let France, which has been the witness of our crimes, be amazed at our repentance. Let us confound all who would imitate our guilt; let us take the side of God against ourselves, and by so doing prevent His judgment. Our former lapses require tears, shame and sorrow to expiate them. Let us offer up these sacrifices from our hearts, let us blush and let us weep. If in these feeble beginnings, O Lord, our hearts are not entirely Thine, let them at least feel that they ought to be so.

Deliver yourself, Héloïse, from the shameful remains of a passion which has taken too deep root. Remember that the least thought for any other than God is an adultery. If you could see me here with my meagre face and melancholy air, surrounded with numbers of persecuting monks, who are alarmed at my reputation for learning and offended at my lean visage, as if I threatened them with a reformation, what would you say of my base sighs and of those unprofitable tears which deceive these credulous men? Alas! I am humbled under love, and not under the Cross. Pity me and free yourself. If your vocation be, as you say, my work, deprive me not of the merit of it by your continual inquietudes. Tell me you will be true to the habit which covers you by an inward retirement. Fear God, that you may be delivered from your frailties; love Him that you may advance in virtue. Be not restless in the cloister for it is the peace of saints. Embrace your bands, they are the chains of Christ Jesus; He will lighten them and bear them with you, if you will but accept them with humility.

Without growing severe to a passion that still possesses you, learn from your own misery to succour your weak sisters; pity them upon consideration of your own faults. And if any thoughts too natural should importune you, fly to the foot of the Cross and there beg for mercy—there are wounds open for healing; lament them before the dying Deity. At the head of a religious society be not a slave, and having rule over queens, begin to govern yourself. Blush at the least revolt of your senses. Remember that even at the foot of the altar we often sacrifice to lying spirits, and that no incense can be more agreeable to them than the earthly passion that still burns in the heart of a religious. If during your abode in the world your soul has acquired a habit of loving, feel it now no more save for Jesus Christ. Repent of all the moments of your life which you have wasted in the world and on pleasure; demand them of me, 'tis a robbery of which I am guilty; take courage and boldly reproach me with it.

I have been indeed your master, but it was only to teach sin. You call me your father; before I had any claim to the title, I deserved that of parricide. I am your brother, but it is the affinity of sin that brings me that distinction. I am called your husband, but it is after a public scandal. If you have abused the sanctity of so many holy terms in the superscription of your letter to do me honour and flatter your own passion, blot them out and replace them with those of murderer, villain and enemy, who has conspired against your honour, troubled your quiet, and betrayed your innocence. You would have perished through my means but for an extraordinary act of grace which, that you might be saved, has thrown me down in the middle of my course.

This is the thought you ought to have of a fugitive who desires to deprive you of the hope of ever seeing him again. But when love has once been sincere how difficult it is to determine to love no more! 'Tis a thousand times more easy to renounce the world than love. I hate this deceitful, faithless world; I think no more of it; but my wandering heart still eternally seeks you, and is filled with anguish at having lost you, in spite of all the powers of my reason. In the meantime, though I should be so cowardly as to retract what you have read, do not suffer me to offer myself to your thoughts save in this last fashion. Remember my last worldly endeavours were to seduce your heart; you perished by my means and I with you: the same waves swallowed us up. We waited for death with indifference, and the same death had carried us headlong to the same punishments. But Providence warded off the blow, and our shipwreck has thrown us into a haven. There are some whom God saves by suffering. Let my salvation be the fruit of your prayers; let me owe it to your tears and your exemplary holiness. Though my heart, Lord, be filled with the love of Thy creature, Thy hand can, when it pleases, empty me of all love save for Thee. To love Héloïse truly is to leave her to that quiet which retirement and virtue afford. I have resolved it: this letter shall be my last fault. Adieu. If I die here I will give orders that my body be carried to the House of the Paraclete. You shall see me in that condition, to demand tears from you, for it will be too late; weep rather for me now and extinguish the fire which burns me. You shall see me in order that your piety may be strengthened by horror of this carcase, and my death be eloquent to tell you what you brave when you love a man. I hope you will be willing, when you have finished this mortal life, to be buried near me. Your cold ashes need then fear nothing, and my tomb shall be the more rich and renowned.

Letter 4:

Héloïse to Abelard

I read the letter I received from you with great impatience: in spite of all my misfortunes I hoped to find nothing in it besides arguments of comfort. But how ingenious are lovers in tormenting themselves. Judge of the exquisite sensibility and force of my love by that which causes the grief of my soul. I was disturbed at the superscription of your letter; why did you place the name of Héloïse before that of Abelard? What means this cruel and unjust distinction? It was your name only—the name of a father and a husband—which my eager eyes sought for. I did not look for my own, which I would if possible forget, for it is the cause of all your misfortunes. The rules of decorum, and your position as master and director over me, opposed that ceremony in addressing me; and love commanded you to banish it: alas! you know all this but too well!

Did you address me thus before cruel fortune had ruined my happiness? I see your heart has forsaken me, and you have made greater advances in the way of devotion than I could wish. Alas! I am too weak to follow you; condescend at least to stay for me and animate me with your advice. Can you have the cruelty to abandon me? The fear of this stabs my heart; the fearful presages you make at the end of your letter, those terrible images you draw of your death, quite distract me. Cruel Abelard! you ought to have stopped my tears and you make them flow. You ought to have quelled the turmoil of my heart and you throw me into greater disorder.

You desire that after your death I should take care of your ashes and pay them the last duties. Alas! in what temper did you conceive these mournful ideas, and how could you describe them to me? Did not the dread of causing my immediate death make the pen drop from your hand? You did not reflect, I suppose, upon all those torments to which you were going to deliver me? Heaven, severe as it has been to me, is not so insensible as to permit me to live one moment after you. Life without Abelard were an insupportable punishment, and death a most exquisite happiness if by that means I could be united to him. If Heaven but hearken to my continual cry, your days will be prolonged and you will bury me.

Is it not your part to prepare me by powerful exhortation against that great crisis which shakes the most resolute and stable minds? Is it not your part to receive my last sighs, superintend my funeral, and give an account of my acts and my faith? Who but you can recommend us worthily to God, and by the fervour and merit of your prayers conduct those souls to Him which you have joined to His worship by solemn vows? We expect those pious offices from your paternal charity. After this you will be free from those disquietudes which now molest you, and you will quit life with ease whenever it shall please God to call you away. You may follow us content with what you have done, and in a full assurance of our happiness. But till then write me no more such terrible things; for we are already sufficiently miserable, nor need to have our sorrows aggravated. Our life here is but a languishing death; would you hasten it? Our present disgraces are sufficient to employ our thoughts continually, and shall we seek in the future new reasons for fear? How void of reason are men, said Seneca, to make distant evils present by reflections, and to take pains before death to lose all the joys of life.

When you have finished your course here below, you said that it is your desire that your body be borne to the House of the Paraclete, to the intent that being always before my eyes you may be ever present in my mind. Can you think that the traces you have drawn on my heart can ever be worn out, or that any length of time can obliterate the memory we hold here of your benefits? And what time shall I find for those prayers you speak of? Alas! I shall then be filled with other cares, for so heavy a misfortune would leave me no moment's quiet. Can my feeble reason resist such powerful assaults? When I am distracted and raving (if I dare say it) even against Heaven itself, I shall not soften it by my cries, but rather provoke it by my reproaches. How should I pray or how bear up against my grief? I should be more eager to follow you

The dread of deaththan to pay you the sad ceremonies of a funeral. It is for you, for Abelard, that I have resolved to live, and if you are ravished from me I can make no use of my miserable days. Alas! what lamentations should I make if Heaven, by a cruel pity, preserved me for that moment? When I but think of this last separation I feel all the pangs of death; what should I be then if I should see this dreadful hour? Forbear therefore to infuse into my mind such mournful thoughts, if not for love, at least for pity.

You desire me to give myself up to my duty, and to be wholly God's, to whom I am consecrated. How can I do that, when you frighten me with apprehensions that continually possess my mind both night and day? When an evil threatens us, and it is impossible to ward it off, why do we give up ourselves to the unprofitable fear of it, which is yet even more tormenting than the evil itself? What have I hope for after the loss of you? What can confine me to earth when death shall have taken away from me all that was dear on it? I have renounced without difficulty all the charms of life, preserving only my love, and the secret pleasure of thinking incessantly of you, and hearing that you live. And yet, alas! you do not live for me, and dare not flatter myself even with the hope that I shall ever see you again. This is the greatest of my afflictions.

Merciless Fortune! hadst thou not persecuted me enough? Thou dost not give me any respite; thou hast exhausted all thy vengeance upon me, and reserved thyself nothing whereby thou mayst appear terrible to others.

Thou hast wearied thyself in tormenting me, and others have nothing to fear from thy anger. But what use to longer arm thyself against me? The wounds I have already received leave no room for others, unless thou desirest to kill me. Or dost thou fear amidst the numerous torments heaped on me, dost thou fear that such a final stroke would deliver me from all other ills? Therefore thou preservest me from death in order to make me die daily.

Dear Abelard, pity my despair! Was ever any being so miserable? The higher you raised me above other women, who envied me your love, the more sensible am I now of the loss of your heart. I was exalted to the top of happiness only that I might have the more terrible fall. Nothing could be compared to my pleasures, and now nothing can equal my misery. My joys once raised the envy of my rivals, my present wretchedness calls forth the compassion of all that see me. My Fortune has been always in extremes; she has loaded me with the greatest favours and then heaped me with the greatest afflictions; ingenious in tormenting me, she has made the memory of the joys I have lost an inexhaustible spring of tears. Love, which being possest was her most delightful gift, on being taken away is an untold sorrow. In short, her malice has entirely succeeded, and I find my present afflictions proportionately bitter as the transports which charmed me were sweet.

But what aggravates my sufferings yet more is, that we began to be miserable at a time when we seemed the least to deserve it. While we gave ourselves up to the enjoyment of a guilty love nothing opposed our pleasures; but scarcely had we retrenched our passion and taken refuge in matrimony, than the wrath of Heaven fell on us with all its weight. And how barbarous was your punishment! Ah! what right had a cruel Uncle over us? We were joined to each other even before the altar, and this should have protected us from the rage of our enemies. Besides, we were separated; you were busy with your lectures and instructed a learned audience in mysteries which the greatest geniuses before you could not penetrate; and I, in obedience to you, retired to a cloister. I there spent whole days in thinking of you, and sometimes meditating on holy lessons to which I endeavoured to apply myself. At this very juncture punishment fell upon us, and you who were least guilty became the object of the whole vengeance of a barbarous man. But why should I rave at Fulbert? I, wretched I, have ruined you, and have been the cause of all your misfortunes. How dangerous it is for a great man to suffer himself to be moved by our sex! He ought from his infancy to be inured to insensibility of heart against all our charms. 'Hearken, my son' (said formerly the wisest of men), attend and keep my instructions; if a beautiful woman by her looks endeavour to entice thee, permit not thyself to be overcome by a corrupt inclination;

reject the poison she offers, and follow not the paths she directs. Her house is the gate of destruction and death.' I have long examined things, and have found that death is less dangerous than beauty. It is the shipwreck of liberty, a fatal snare, from which it is impossible ever to get free. It was a woman who threw down the first man from the glorious position in which Heaven had placed him; she, who was created to partake of his happiness, was the sole cause of his ruin. How bright had been the glory of Samson if his heart had been proof against the charms of Delilah, as against the weapons of the Philistines. A woman disarmed and betrayed he who had been a conqueror of armies. He saw himself delivered into the hands of his enemies; he was deprived of his eyes, those inlets of love into the soul; distracted and despairing he died without any consolation save that of including his enemies in his ruin. Solomon, that he might please women, forsook pleasing God; that king whose wisdom princes came from all parts to admire, he whom God had chosen to build the temple, abandoned the worship of the very altars he had raised, and proceeded to such a pitch of folly as even to burn incense to idols. Job had no enemy more cruel than his wife; what temptations did he not bear? The evil spirit who had declared himself his persecutor employed a woman as an instrument to shake his constancy. And the same evil spirit made Héloïse an instrument to ruin Abelard. All the poor comfort I have is that I am not the voluntary cause of your misfortunes. I have not betrayed you; but my constancy and love have been destructive to you. If I have committed a crime in loving you so constantly I cannot repent it. I have endeavoured to please you even at the expense of my virtue, and therefore deserve the pains I feel. As soon as I was persuaded of your love I delayed scarce a moment in yielding to your protestations; to be beloved by Abelard was in my esteem so great a glory, and I so impatiently desired it, not to believe in it immediately. I aimed at nothing but convincing you of my utmost passion. I made no use of those defences of disdain and honour; those enemies of pleasure which tyrannise over our sex made in me but a weak and unprofitable resistance. I sacrificed all to my love, and I forced my duty to give place to the ambition of making happy the most famous and learned person of the age. If any consideration had been able to stop me, it would have been without doubt my love. I feared lest having nothing further to offer you your passion might become languid, and you might seek for new pleasures in another conquest. But it was easy for you to cure me of a suspicion so opposite to my own inclination. I ought to have foreseen other more certain evils, and to have considered that the idea of lost enjoyments would be the trouble of my whole life.

How happy should I be could I wash out with my tears the memory of those pleasures which I yet think of with delight. At least I will try by strong endeavour to smother in my heart those desires to which the frailty of my nature gives birth, and I will exercise on myself such torments as those you have to suffer from the rage of your enemies. I will endeavour by this means to satisfy you at least, if I cannot appease an angry God. For to show you to what a deplorable condition I am reduced, and how far my repentance is from being complete, I dare even accuse Heaven at this moment of cruelty for delivering you over to the snares prepared for you. My repinings can only kindle divine wrath, when I should be seeking for mercy.

In order to expiate a crime it is not sufficient to bear the punishment; whatever we suffer is of no avail if the passion still continues and the heart is filled with the same desire. It is an easy matter to confess a weakness, and inflict on ourselves some punishment, but it needs perfect power over our nature to extinguish the memory of pleasures, which by a loved habitude have gained possession of our minds. How many persons do we see who make an outward confession of their faults, yet, far from being in distress about them, take a new pleasure in relating them. Contrition of the heart ought to accompany the confession of the mouth, yet this very rarely happens. I, who have experienced so many pleasures in loving you, feel, in spite of myself, that I cannot repent them, nor forbear through memory to enjoy them over again. Whatever efforts I use, on whatever side I turn, the sweet thought still pursues me, and every object brings to my mind what it is my duty to forget. During the quiet night, when my heart ought to be still in that sleep which suspends the greatest cares, I cannot avoid the illusions of my heart. I dream I am still with my dear Abelard. I see him, I speak to him and hear him answer. Charmed with each other we forsake our studies and give ourselves up to love. Sometimes too I seem to struggle with your enemies; I oppose their fury, I break into piteous cries, and in a moment I awake in tears. Even into holy places before the altar I carry the memory of our love, and far from lamenting for having been seduced by pleasures, I sigh for having lost them.

I remember (for nothing is forgot by lovers) the time and place in which you first declared your passion and swore you would love me till death. Your words, your oaths, are deeply graven in my heart. My stammering speech betrays to all the disorder of my mind; my sighs discover me, and your name is ever on my lips. O Lord! when I am thus afflicted why dost not Thou pity my weakness and strengthen me with Thy grace? You are happy, Abelard, in that grace is given you, and your misfortune has been the occasion of your finding rest. The punishment of your body has cured the deadly wounds of your soul. The tempest has driven you into the haven. God, who seemed to deal heavily with you, sought only to help you; He was a Father chastising and not an Enemy revenging—a wise Physician putting you to some pain in order to preserve your life. I am a thousand times more to be pitied than you, for I have still a thousand passions to fight. I must resist those fires which love kindles in a young heart. Our sex is nothing but weakness, and I have the greater difficulty in defending myself because the enemy that attacks me pleases me; I doat on the danger which threatens; how then can I avoid yielding?

In the midst of these struggles I try at least to conceal my weakness from those you have entrusted to my care. All who are about me admire my virtue, but could their eyes penetrate, into my heart what would they not discover? My passions there are in rebellion; I preside over others but cannot rule myself. I have a false covering, and this seeming virtue is a real vice. Men judge me praiseworthy, but I am guilty before God; from His all-seeing eye nothing is hid, and He views through all their windings the secrets of the heart. I cannot escape His discovery. And yet it means great effort to me merely to maintain this appearance of virtue, so surely this troublesome hypocrisy is in some sort commendable. I give no scandal to the world which is so easy to take bad impressions; I do not shake the virtue of those feeble ones who are under my rule. With my heart full of the love of man, I teach them at least to love only God. Charmed with the pomp of worldly pleasures, I endeavour to show them that they are all vanity and deceit. I have just strength enough to conceal from them my longings, and I look upon that as a great effect of grace. If it is not enough to make me embrace virtue, 'tis enough to keep me from committing sin.

And yet it is in vain to try and separate these two things: they must be guilty who are not righteous, and they depart from virtue who delay to approach it. Besides, we ought to have no other motive than the love of God. Alas! what can I then hope for? I own to my confusion I fear more to offend a man than to provoke God, and I study less to please Him than to please you. Yes, it was your command only, and not a sincere vocation, which sent me into these cloisters; I sought to give you ease and not to sanctify myself. How unhappy am I! I tear myself from all that pleases me; I bury myself alive; I exercise myself with the most rigid fastings and all those severities the cruel laws impose on us; I feed myself with tears and sorrows; and notwithstanding this I merit nothing by my penance. My false piety has long deceived you as well as others; you have thought me at peace when I was more disturbed than ever. You persuaded yourself I was wholly devoted to my duty, yet I had no business but love. Under this mistake you desire my prayers—alas! I need yours! Do not presume upon my virtue and my care; I am wavering, fix me by your advice; I am feeble, sustain and guide me by your counsel.

What occasion had you to praise me? Praise is often hurtful for those on whom it is bestowed: a secret vanity springs up in the heart, blinds us, and conceals from us the wounds that are half healed. A seducer flatters us, and at the same time destroys us. A sincere friend disguises nothing from us, and far from passing a light hand over the wound, makes us feel it the more intensely by applying remedies. Why do you not deal after this manner with me? Will you be esteemed a base, dangerous flatterer? or if you chance to see anything commendable in me, have you no fear that vanity, which is so natural to all women, should quite efface it? But let us not judge of virtue by outward appearances, for then the reprobate as well as the elect may lay claim to it. An artful impostor may by his address gain more admiration than is given to the zeal of a saint.

The heart of man is a labyrinth whose windings are very difficult to discover. The praises you give me are the more dangerous because I love the person who bestows them. The more I desire to please you the readier am I to believe the merit you attribute to me. Ah! think rather how to nerve my weakness by wholesome remonstrances! Be rather fearful than confident of my salvation; say our virtue is founded upon weakness, and that they only will be crowned who have fought with the greatest difficulties. But I seek not the crown which is the reward of victory I am content if I can avoid danger. It is easier to keep out of the way than to win a battle. There are several degrees in glory, and I am not ambitious of the highest; I leave them to those of greater courage who have often been victorious. I seek not to conquer for fear I should be overcome; happiness enough for me to escape shipwreck and at last reach port. Heaven commands me to renounce my fatal passion for you, but oh! my heart will never be able to consent to it. Adieu.

Letter 5:

Héloïse to Abelard

Dear Abelard,—You expect, perhaps, that I should accuse you of negligence. You have not answered my last letter, and thanks to Heaven, in the condition I am now in it is a relief to me that you show so much insensibility for the passion which I betrayed. At last, Abelard, you have lost Héloïse for ever. Notwithstanding all the oaths I made to think of nothing but you, and to be entertained by nothing but you, I have banished you from my thoughts, I have forgot you. Thou charming idea of a lover I once adored, thou wilt be no more my happiness! Dear image of Abelard! thou wilt no longer follow me, no longer shall I remember thee. O celebrity and merit of that man who, in spite of his enemies, is the wonder of the age! O enchanting pleasures to which Héloïse resigned herself—you, you have been my tormentors! I confess my inconstancy, Abelard, without a blush; let my infidelity teach the world that there is no depending on the promises of women—we are all subject to change. This troubles you, Abelard; this news without surprises you; you never imagined Héloïse could be inconstant. She was prejudiced by such a strong inclination towards you that you cannot conceive how Time could alter it. But be undeceived, I am going to disclose to you my falseness, though, instead of reproaching me, I persuade myself you will shed tears of joy. When I tell you what Rival hath ravished my heart from you, you will praise my inconstancy, and pray this Rival to fix it. By this you will know that 'tis God alone that takes Héloïse from you. Yes, my dear Abelard, He gives my mind that tranquillity which a vivid remembrance of our misfortunes formerly forbade. Just Heaven! what other rival could take me from you? Could you imagine it possible for a mere human to blot you from my heart? Could you think me guilty of sacrificing the virtuous and learned Abelard to any other but God? No, I believe you have done me justice on this point. I doubt not you are eager to learn what means God used to accomplish so great an end? I will tell you, that you may wonder at the secret ways of Providence. Some few days after you sent me your last letter I fell dangerously ill; the physicians gave me over, and I expected certain death. Then it was that my passion, which always before seemed innocent, grew criminal in my eyes. My memory represented faithfully to me all the past actions of my life, and I confess to you pain for our love was the only pain I felt. Death, which till then I had only viewed from a distance, now presented itself to me as it appears to sinners. I began to dread the wrath of God now I was near experiencing it, and I repented that I had not better used the means of Grace. Those tender letters I wrote to you, those fond conversations I have had with you, give me as much pain now as they had formerly given pleasure. 'Ah, miserable Héloïse!' I said, 'if it is a crime to give oneself up to such transports, and if, after this life is ended, punishment certainly follows them, why didst thou not resist such dangerous temptations? Think on the tortures prepared for thee, consider with terror the store of torments, and recollect, at the same time, those pleasures which thy deluded soul thought so entrancing. Ah! dost thou not despair for having rioted in such false pleasures?' In short, Abelard, imagine all the remorse of mind I suffered, and you will not be astonished at my change.

Solitude is insupportable to the uneasy mind; its troubles increase in the midst of silence, and retirement heightens them. Since I have been shut up in these walls I have done nothing but weep our misfortunes. This cloister has resounded with my cries, and, like a wretch condemned to eternal slavery, I have worn out my days with grief. Instead of fulfilling God's merciful design towards me I have offended against Him; I have looked upon this sacred refuge as a frightful prison, and have borne with unwillingness the yoke of the Lord. Instead of purifying myself with a life of penitence I have confirmed my condemnation. What a fatal mistake! But, Abelard, I have torn off the bandage which blinded me, and, if I dare rely upon my own feelings, I have now made myself worthy of your esteem, You are to me no more the loving Abelard who constantly sought private conversations with me by deceiving the vigilance of our observers. Our misfortunes gave you a horror of vice, and you instantly consecrated the rest of your days to virtue, and seemed to submit willingly to the necessity. I indeed, more tender than you, and more sensible to pleasure, bore misfortune with extreme impatience, and you have heard my exclaimings against your enemies. You have seen my resentment in my late letters; it was this, doubtless, which deprived me of the esteem of my Abelard. You were alarmed at my repinings, and, if the truth be told, despaired of my salvation. You could not foresee that Héloïse would conquer so reigning a passion; but you were mistaken, Abelard, my weakness, when supported by grace, has not hindered me from winning a complete victory. Restore me, then, to your esteem; your own piety should solicit you to this.

But what secret trouble rises in my soul—what unthought-of emotion now rises to oppose the resolution I have formed to sigh no more for Abelard? Just Heaven! have I not triumphed over my love? Unhappy Héloïse! as long as thou drawest a breath it is decreed thou must love Abelard. Weep, unfortunate wretch, for thou never hadst a more just occasion. I ought to die of grief; grace had overtaken me and I had promised to be faithful to it, but now am I perjured once more, and even grace is sacrificed to Abelard. This sacrilege fills up the measure of my iniquity. After this how can I hope that God will open to me the treasure of His mercy, for I have tired out His forgiveness. I began to offend Him from the first moment I saw Abelard; an unhappy sympathy engaged us both in a guilty love, and God raised us up an enemy to separate us. I lament the misfortune which lighted upon us and I adore the cause. Ah! I ought rather to regard this misfortune as the gift of Heaven, which disapproved of our engagement and parted us, and I ought to apply myself to extirpate my passion. How much better it were to forget entirely the object of it than to preserve a memory so fatal to my peace and salvation? Great God! shall Abelard possess my thoughts for ever? Can I never free myself from the chains of love? But perhaps I am unreasonably afraid; virtue directs all my acts and they are all subject to grace. Therefore fear not, Abelard; I have no longer those sentiments which being described in my letters have occasioned you so much trouble. I will no more endeavour, by the relation of those pleasures our passion gave us, to awaken any guilty fondness you may yet feel for me. I free you from all your oaths; forget the titles of lover and husband and keep only that of father. I expect no more from you than tender protestations and those letters so proper to feed the flame of love. I demand nothing of you but spiritual advice and wholesome discipline. The path of holiness, however thorny it be, will yet appear agreeable to me if I may but walk in your footsteps. You will always find me ready to follow you. I shall read with more pleasure the letters in which you shall describe the advantages of virtue than ever I did those in which you so artfully instilled the poison of passion. You cannot now be silent without a crime. When I was possessed with so violent a love, and pressed you so earnestly to write to me,

God holds her hearthow many letters did I send you before I could obtain one from you? You denied me in my misery the only comfort which was left me, because you thought it pernicious. You endeavoured by severities to force me to forget you, nor do I blame you; but now you have nothing to fear. This fortunate illness, with which Providence has chastised me for my good, has done what all human efforts and your cruelty in vain attempted. I see now the vanity of that happiness we had set our hearts upon, as if it were eternal. What fears, what distress have we not suffered for it!

No, Lord, there is no pleasure upon earth but that which virtue gives. The heart amidst all worldly delights feels a sting; it is uneasy and restless until fixed on Thee. What have I not suffered, Abelard, whilst I kept alive in my retirement those fires which ruined me in the world? I saw with hatred the walls that surrounded me; the hours seemed as long as years. I repented a thousand times that I had buried myself here. But since grace has opened my eyes all the scene is changed; solitude looks charming, and the peace of the place enters my very heart. In the satisfaction of doing my duty I feel a delight above all that riches, pomp or sensuality could afford. My quiet has indeed cost me dear, for I have bought it at the price of my love; I have offered a violent sacrifice I thought beyond my power. But if I have torn you from my heart, be not jealous; God, who ought always to have possessed it, reigns there in your stead. Be content with having a place in my mind which you shall never lose; I shall always take a secret pleasure in thinking of you, and esteem it a glory to obey those rules you shall give me.

This very moment I receive a letter from you; I will read it and answer it immediately. You shall see by my promptitude in writing to you that you are always dear to me.

You very obligingly reproach me for delay in writing you any news; my illness must excuse that. I omit no opportunities of giving you marks of my remembrance. I thank you for the uneasiness you say my silence caused you, and the kind fears you express concerning my health. Yours, you tell me, is but weakly, and you thought lately you should have died. With what indifference, cruel man, do you tell me a thing so certain to afflict me? I told you in my former letter how unhappy I should be if you died, and if you love me you will moderate the rigours of your austere life. I represented to you the occasion I had for your advice, and consequently the reason there was you should take care of yourself;—but I will not tire you with repetitions. You desire us not to forget you in our prayers: ah! dear Abelard, you may depend upon the zeal of this society; it is devoted to you and you cannot justly fear its forgetfulness. You are our Father, and we are your children; you are our guide, and we resign ourselves to your direction with full assurance in your piety. You command; we obey; we faithfully execute what you have prudently ordered. We impose no penance on ourselves but what you recommend, lest we should rather follow an indiscreet zeal than solid virtue. In a word, nothing is thought right but what has Abelard's approbation. You tell me one thing that perplexes me that you have heard that some of our Sisters are bad examples, and that they are generally not strict enough. Ought this to seem strange to you who know how monasteries are filled nowadays? Do fathers consult the inclination of their children when they settle them? Are not interest and policy their only rules? This is the reason that monasteries are often filled with those who are a scandal to them. But I conjure you to tell me what are the irregularities you have heard of, and to show me the proper remedy for them. I have not yet observed any looseness: when I have I will take due care. I walk my rounds every night and make those I catch abroad return to their chambers; for I remember all the adventures that happened in the monasteries near Paris.

You end your letter with a general deploring of your unhappiness and wish for death to end a weary life. Is it possible so great a genius as you cannot rise above your misfortunes? What would the world say should they read the letters you send me? Would they consider the noble motive of your retirement or not rather think you had shut yourself up merely to lament your woes? What would your young students say, who come so far to hear you and prefer your severe lectures to the ease of a worldly life, if they should discover you secretly a slave to your passions and the victim of those weaknesses from which your rule secures them? This Abelard they so much admire, this great leader, would lose his fame and become the sport of his pupils.

If these reasons are not sufficient to give you constancy in your misfortune, cast your eyes upon me, and admire the resolution with which I shut myself up at your request. I was young when we separated, and (if I dare believe what you were always telling me) worthy of any man's affections. If I had loved nothing in Abelard but sensual pleasure, other men might have comforted me upon my loss of him. You know what I have done, excuse me therefore from repeating it; think of those assurances I gave you of loving you still with the utmost tenderness. I dried your tears with kisses, and because you were less powerful I became less reserved. Ah! if you had loved with delicacy, the oaths I made, the transports I indulged, the caresses I gave, would surely have comforted you. Had you seen me grow by degrees indifferent to you, you might have had reason to despair, but you never received greater tokens of my affection than after you felt misfortune.

Let me see no more in your letters, dear Abelard, such murmurs against Fate; you are not the only one who has felt her blows and you ought to forget her outrages. What a shame it is that a philosopher cannot accept what might befall any man. Govern yourself by my example; I was born with violent passions, I daily strive with tender emotions, and glory in triumphing and subjecting them to reason. Must a weak mind fortify one that is so much superior? But I am carried away. Is it thus I write to nay dear Abelard? He who practises all those virtues he preaches? If you complain of Fortune, it is not so much that you feel her strokes as that you try to show your enemies how much to blame they are in attempting to hurt you. Leave them, Abelard, to exhaust their malice, and continue to charm your auditors. Discover those treasures of learning Heaven seems to have reserved for you; your enemies, struck with the splendour of your reasoning, will in the end do you justice. How happy should I be could I see all the world as entirely persuaded of your probity as I am. Your learning is allowed by all; your greatest adversaries confess you are ignorant of nothing the mind of man is capable of knowing.

My dear Husband (for the last time I use that title!), shall I never see you again? Shall I never have the pleasure of embracing you before death? What dost thou say, wretched Héloïse? Dost thou know what thou desirest? Couldst thou behold those brilliant eyes without recalling the tender glances which have been so fatal to thee? Couldst thou see that majestic air of Abelard without being jealous of everyone who beholds so attractive a man? That mouth cannot be looked upon without desire; in short, no woman can view the person of Abelard without danger. Ask no more therefore to see Abelard; if the memory of him has caused thee so much trouble, Héloïse, what would not his presence

47

do? What desires will it not excite in thy soul? How will it be possible to keep thy reason at the sight of so lovable a man?

I will own to you what makes the greatest pleasure in my retirement; after having passed the day in thinking of you, full of the repressed idea, I give myself up at night to sleep. Then it is that Héloïse, who dares not think of you by day, resigns herself with pleasure to see and hear you. How my eyes gloat over you! Sometimes you tell me stories of your secret troubles, and create in me a felt sorrow; sometimes the rage of our enemies is forgotten and you press me to you and I yield to you, and our souls, animated with the same passion, are sensible of the same pleasures. But O! delightful dreams and tender illusions, how soon do you vanish away! I awake and open my eyes to find no Abelard: I stretch out my arms to embrace him and he is not there; I cry, and he hears me not. What a fool I am to tell my dreams to you who are insensible to these pleasures. But do you, Abelard, never see Héloïse in your sleep? How does she appear to you? Do you entertain her with the same tender language as formerly, and are you glad or sorry when you awake? Pardon me, Abelard, pardon a mistaken lover. I must no longer expect from you that vivacity which once marked your every action; no more must I require from you the correspondence of desires. We have bound ourselves to severe austerities and must follow them at all costs. Let us think of our duties and our rules, and make good use of that necessity which keeps us separate. You, Abelard, will happily finish your course; your desires and ambitions will be no obstacle to your salvation. But Héloïse must weep, she must lament for ever without being certain whether all her tears will avail for her salvation.

I had liked to have ended my letter without telling you what happened here a few days ago. A young nun, who had been forced to enter the convent without a vocation therefor, is by a stratagem I know nothing of escaped and fled to England with a gentleman. I have ordered all the house to conceal the matter. Ah, Abelard! if you were near us these things would not happen, for all the Sisters, charmed with seeing and hearing you, would think of nothing but practising your rules and directions. The young nun had never formed so criminal a design as that of breaking her vows had you been at our head to exhort us to live in holiness. If your eyes were witnesses of our actions they would be innocent. When we slipped you should lift us up and establish us by your counsels; we should march with sure steps in the rough path of virtue. I begin to perceive, Abelard, that I take too much pleasure in writing to you; I ought to burn this letter. It shows that I still feel a deep passion for you, though at the beginning I tried to persuade you to the contrary. I am sensible of waves both of grace and passion, and by turns yield to each. Have pity, Abelard, on the condition to which you have brought me, and make in some measure my last days as peaceful as my first have been uneasy and disturbed.

Letter 6:

Abelard to Héloïse

Write no more to me, Héloïse, write no more to me; 'tis time to end communications which make our penances of nought avail. We retired from the world to purify ourselves, and, by a conduct directly contrary to Christian morality, we became odious to Jesus Christ. Let us no more deceive ourselves with remembrance of our past pleasures; we but make our lives troubled and spoil the sweets of solitude. Let us make good use of our austerities and no longer preserve the memories of our crimes amongst the severities of penance. Let a mortification of body and mind, a strict fasting, continual solitude, profound and holy meditations, and a sincere love of God succeed our former irregularities.

Let us try to carry religious perfection to its farthest point. It is beautiful to find Christian minds so disengaged from earth, from the creatures and themselves, that they seem to act independently of those bodies they are joined to, and to use them as their slaves. We can never raise ourselves to too great heights when God is our object. Be our efforts ever so great they will always come short of attaining that exalted Divinity which even our apprehension cannot reach. Let us act for God's glory independent of the creatures or ourselves, paying no regard to our own desires or the opinions of others. Were we in this temper of mind, Héloïse, I would willingly make my abode at the Paraclete, and by my earnest care for the house I have founded draw a thousand blessings on it. I would instruct it by my words and animate it by my example: I would watch over the lives of my Sisters, and would command nothing but what I myself would perform: I would direct you to pray, meditate, labour, and keep vows of silence; and I would myself pray, labour, meditate, and be silent.

And when I spoke it should be to lift you up when you should fall, to strengthen you in your weaknesses, to enlighten you in that darkness and obscurity which might at any time surprise you. I would comfort you under the severities used by persons of great virtue: I would moderate the vivacity of your zeal and piety and give your virtue an even temperament: I would point out those duties you ought to perform, and satisfy those doubts which through the weakness of your reason might arise. I would be your master and father, and by a marvellous talent I would become lively or slow, gentle or severe, according to the different characters of those I should guide in the painful path to Christian perfection.

But whither does my vain imagination carry me! Ah, Héloïse, how far are we from such a happy temper? Your heart still burns with that fatal fire you cannot extinguish, and mine is full of trouble and unrest. Think not, Héloïse, that I here enjoy a perfect peace; I will for the last time open my heart to you;— I am not yet disengaged from you, and though I fight against my excessive tenderness for you, in spite of all my endeavours I remain but too sensible of your sorrows and long to share in them. Your letters have indeed moved me; I could not read with indifference characters written by that dear hand! I sigh and weep, and all my reason is scarce sufficient to conceal my weakness from my pupils. This, unhappy Héloïse, is the miserable condition of Abelard. The world, which is generally wrong in its notions, thinks I am at peace, and imagining that I loved you only for the gratification of the senses, have now forgot you. What a mistake is this! People indeed were not wrong in saying that when we separated it was shame and grief that made me abandon the world. It was not, as you know, a sincere repentance for having offended God which inspired me with a design for retiring. However, I consider our misfortunes as a secret design of Providence to punish our sins; and only look upon Fulbert as the instrument of divine vengeance. Grace drew me into an asylum where I might yet have remained if the rage of my enemies would have permitted; I have endured all their persecutions, not doubting that God Himself raised them up in order to purify me.

When He saw me perfectly obedient to His Holy Will, He permitted that I should justify my doctrine; I made its purity public, and showed in the end that my faith was not only orthodox, but also perfectly clear from all suspicion of novelty.

I should be happy if I had none to fear but my enemies, and no other hindrance to my salvation but their calumny. But, Héloïse, you to strive make me tremble, your letters declare to me that you are enslaved to human love, and yet, if you cannot conquer it, you cannot be saved; and what part would you have me play in this trial? Would you have me stifle the inspirations of the Holy Ghost? Shall I, to soothe you, dry up those tears which the Evil Spirit makes you shed—shall this be the fruit of my meditations? No, let us be more firm in our resolutions; we have not retired save to lament our sins and to gain heaven; let us then resign ourselves to God with all our heart.

I know everything is difficult in the beginning; but it is glorious to courageously start a great action, and glory increases proportionately as the difficulties are more considerable. We ought on this account to surmount bravely all obstacles which might hinder us in the practice of Christian virtue. In a monastery men are proved as gold in a furnace. No one can continue long there unless he bear worthily the yoke of the Lord.

Attempt to break those shameful chains which bind you to the flesh, and if by the assistance of grace you are so happy as to accomplish this, I entreat you to think of me in your prayers. Endeavour with all your strength to be the pattern of a perfect Christian; it is difficult, I confess, but not impossible; and I expect this beautiful triumph from your teachable disposition. If your first efforts prove weak do not give way to despair, for that would be cowardice; besides, I would have you know that you must necessarily take great pains, for you strive to conquer a terrible enemy, to extinguish a raging fire, to reduce to subjection your dearest affections. You have to fight against your own desires, so be not pressed down with the weight of your corrupt nature. You have to do with a cunning adversary who will use all means to seduce you; be always upon your guard. While we live we are exposed to temptations; this made a great saint say, 'The life of man is one long temptation': the devil, who never sleeps, walks continually around us in order to surprise us on some unguarded side, and enters into our soul in order to destroy it.

However perfect anyone may be, yet he may fall into temptations, and perhaps into such as may be useful. Nor is it wonderful that man should never be exempt from them, because he always hath in himself their source; scarce are we delivered from one temptation when another attacks us. Such is the lot of the posterity of Adam, that they should always have something to suffer, because they have forfeited their primitive happiness. We vainly flatter ourselves that we shall conquer temptations by flying; if we join not patience and humility we shall torment ourselves to no purpose. We shall more certainly compass our end by imploring God's assistance than by using any means of our own.

Be constant, Héloïse, and trust in God; then you shall fall into few temptations: when they come stifle them at their birth—let them not take root in your heart. 'Apply remedies to a disease,' said an ancient, 'at the beginning, for when it hath gained strength medicines are of no avail': temptations have their degrees, they are at first mere thoughts and do not appear dangerous; the imagination receives them without any fears; the pleasure grows; we dwell upon it, and at last we yield to it.

Do you now, Héloïse, applaud my design of making you walk in the steps of the saints? Do my words give you any relish for penitence? Have you not remorse for your wanderings, and do you not wish you could, like Magdalen, wash our Saviour's feet with your tears? If you have not yet these ardent aspirations, pray that you may be inspired by them. I shall never cease to recommend you in my prayers and to beseech God to assist you in your design of dying holily. You have quitted the world, and what object was worthy to detain you there? Lift up your eyes always to Him to whom the rest of your days are consecrated. Life upon this earth is misery; the very necessities to which our bodies are subject here are matters of affliction to a saint. 'Lord,' said the royal prophet, 'deliver me from my necessities.' Many are wretched who do not know they are; and yet they are more wretched who know their misery and yet cannot hate the corruption of the age. What fools are men to engage themselves to earthly things! They will be undeceived one day, and will know too late how much they have been to blame in loving such false good. Truly pious persons are not thus mistaken; they are freed from all sensual pleasures and raise their desires to Heaven.

Begin, Héloïse; put your design into action without delay; you have yet time enough to work out your salvation. Love Christ, and despise yourself for His sake; He will possess your heart and be the sole object of your sighs and tears; seek for no comfort but in Him. If you do not free yourself from me, you will fall with me; but if you leave me and cleave to Him, you will be steadfast and safe. If you force the Lord to forsake you, you will fall into trouble; but if you are faithful to Him you shall find joy. Magdalen wept, thinking that Jesus had forsaken her, but Martha said, 'See, the Lord calls you.' Be diligent in your duty, obey faithfully the calls of grace, and Jesus will be with you. Attend, Héloïse, to some instructions I have to give you: you are at the head of a society, and you know there is a difference between those who lead a private life and those who are charged with the conduct of others: the first need only labour for their own sanctification, and in their round of duties are not obliged to practise all the virtues in such an apparent manner: but those who have the charge of others entrusted to them ought by their example to encourage their followers to do all the good of which they are capable. I beseech you to remember this truth, and so to follow it that your whole life may be a perfect model of that of a religious recluse.

God heartily desires our salvation, and has made all the means of it easy to us. In the Old Testament He has written in the tables of law what He requires of us, that we might not be bewildered in seeking after His will. In the New Testament He has written the law of grace to the intent that it might ever be present in our hearts; so, knowing the weakness and incapacity of our nature, He has given us grace to perform His will. And, as if this were not enough, He has raised up at all times, in all states of the Church, men who by their exemplary life can excite others to their duty. To effect this He has chosen persons of every age, sex and condition. Strive now to unite in yourself all the virtues of these different examples. Have the purity of virgins, the austerity of anchorites, the zeal of pastors and bishops, and the constancy of martyrs. Be exact in the course of your whole life to fulfil the duties of a holy and enlightened superior, and then death, which is commonly considered as terrible, will appear agree- able to you.

'The death of His saints,' says the prophet, 'is precious in the sight of the Lord.' Nor is it difficult to discover why their death should have this advantage over that of sinners. I have remarked three things which might have given the prophet an occasion of speaking thus:—First, their resignation to the will of God; second, the continuation of their good works; and lastly, the triumph they gain over the devil.

A saint who has accustomed himself to submit to the will of God yields to death without reluctance. He waits with joy (says Dr. Gregory) for the Judge who is to reward him; he fears not to quit this miserable mortal life in order to begin an immortal happy one. It is not so with the sinner, says the same Father; he fears, and with reason, he trembles at the approach of the least sickness; death is terrible to him because he dreads the presence of the offended Judge; and having so often abused the means of grace he sees no way to avoid the punishment of his sins.

The saints have also this advantage over sinners, that having become familiar with works of piety of during their life they exercise them without trouble, and having gained new strength against the devil every time they overcame him, they will find themselves in a condition at the hour of death to obtain that victory on which depends all eternity, and the blessed union of their souls with their Creator.

I hope, Héloïse, that after having deplored the irregularities of your past life, you will 'die the death of the righteous.' Ah, how few there are who make this end! And why? It is because there are so few who love the Cross of Christ. Everyone wishes to be saved, but few will use those means which religion prescribes. Yet can we be saved by nothing but the Cross: why then refuse to bear it? Hath not our Saviour bore it before us, and died for us, to the end that we might also bear it and desire to die also? All the saints have suffered affliction, and our Saviour himself did not pass one hour of His life without some sorrow. Hope not therefore to be exempt from suffering: the Cross, Héloïse, is always at hand, take care that you do not receive it with regret, for by so doing you will make it more heavy and you will he oppressed by it to no profit. On the contrary, if you bear it with willing courage, all your sufferings will create in you a holy confidence whereby you will find comfort in God. Hear our Saviour who says, 'My child, renounce yourself, take up your Cross and follow Me. Oh, Héloïse, do you doubt? Is not your soul ravished at so saving a command? Are you insensible to words so full of kindness? Beware, Héloïse, of refusing a Husband who demands you, and who is more to be feared than any earthly lover. Provoked at your contempt and ingratitude, He will turn His love into anger and make you feel His vengeance. How will you sustain His presence when you shall stand before His tribunal? He will reproach you for having despised His grace, He will represent to you His sufferings for you. What answer can you make? He will then be implacable: He will say to you, 'Go, proud creature, and dwell in everlasting flames. I separated you from the world to purify you in solitude and you did not second my design. I endeavoured to save you and you wilfully destroyed yourself; go, wretch, and take the portion of the reprobates.'

Oh, Héloïse, prevent these terrible words, and avoid, by a holy life, the punishment prepared for sinners. I dare not give you a description of those dreadful torments which are the consequences of a career of guilt. I am filled with horror when they offer themselves to my imagination. And yet, Héloïse, I can conceive nothing which can reach the tortures of the damned; the fire which we see upon this earth is but the shadow of that which burns them; and without enumerating their endless pains, the loss of God which they feel increases all their torments. Can anyone sin who is persuaded of this? My God! can we dare to offend Thee? Though the riches of Thy mercy could not engage us to love Thee, the dread of being thrown into such an abyss of misery should restrain us from doing anything which might displease Thee.

The hope of heaven I question not, Héloïse, but you will hereafter apply yourself in good earnest to the business of your salvation; this ought to be your whole concern. Banish me, therefore, for ever from your heart—it is the best advice I can give you, for the remembrance of a person we have loved guiltily cannot but be hurtful, whatever advances we may have made in the way of virtue. When you have extirpated your unhappy inclination towards me, the practice of every virtue will become easy; and when at last your life is conformable to that of Christ, death will be desirable to you. Your soul will joyfully leave this body, and direct its flight to heaven. Then you will appear with confidence before your Saviour; you will not read your reprobation written in the judgment book, but you will hear your Saviour say, Come, partake of My glory, and enjoy the eternal reward I have appointed for those virtues you have practised.

Farewell, Héloïse, this is the last advice of your dear Abelard; for the last time let me persuade you to follow the rules of the Gospel. Heaven grant that your heart, once so sensible of my love, may now yield to be directed by my zeal. May the idea of your loving Abelard, always present to your mind, be now changed into the image of Abelard truly penitent; and may you shed as many tears for your salvation as you have done for our misfortunes.

Alexander Pope's 'Eloisa to Abelard'

In these deep solitudes and awful cells,
Where heav'nly-pensive contemplation dwells,
And ever-musing melancholy reigns;
What means this tumult in a Vestal's veins?
Why rove my thoughts beyond this last retreat?
Why feels my heart its long-forgotten heat?
Yet, yet I love!—From Abelard it came,
And Eloïsa yet must kiss the name.
  Dear fatal name! rest ever unrevealed,
Nor pass these lips in holy silence sealed:
Hide it, my heart, within that close disguise,
Where mix'd with God's, his lov'd Idea lies:
O write it not my hand—the name appears
Already written—wash it out, my tears!
In vain lost Eloïsa weeps and prays.
Her heart still dictates, and her hand obeys.
  Relentless walls! whose darksome round contains
Repentant sighs, and voluntary pains;
Ye rugged rock! which holy knees have worn;
Ye grots and caverns shagg'd with horrid thorn!
Shrines! where their vigils pale-ey'd virgins keep,
And pitying saints, whose statues learn to weep!
Tho' cold like you, unmov'd and silent grown,
I have not yet forgot myself to stone.
All is not Heav'n's while Abelard has part,
Still rebel nature holds out half my heart;
Nor pray'rs nor fasts its stubborn pulse restrain,
Nor tears for ages taught to flow in vain.
  Soon as thy letters trembling I unclose,
That well-known name awakens all my woes.
O name for ever sad! for ever dear!
Still breath'd in sighs, still usher'd with a tear.
I tremble too, where'er my own I find,
Some dire misfortune follows close behind.

Line after line my gushing eyes o'erflow,
Led thro' a sad variety of woe:
Now warm in love, now with'ring in my bloom,
Lost in a convent's solitary gloom!
There stern Religion quench'd th' unwilling flame,
There died the best of passions, Love and Fame.
  Yet write, oh write me all, that I may join
Griefs to thy griefs, and echo sighs to thine.
Nor foes nor fortune take this pow'r away;
And is my Abelard less kind than they?
Tears still are mine, and those I need not spare,
Love but demands what else were shed in pray'r;
No happier task these faded eyes pursue:
To read and weep is all they now can do.
  Then share thy pain, allow that sad relief;
Ah, more than share it, give me all thy grief.
Heav'n first taught letters for some wretch's aid,
Some banish'd lover, or some captive maid;
They live, they speak, they breathe what love inspires,
Warm from the soul, and faithful to its fires,
The virgin's wish without her fears impart,
Excuse the blush, and pour out all the heart,
Speed the soft intercourse from soul to soul,
And waft a sigh from Indus to the Pole.
  Thou know'st how guiltless first I met thy flame,
When Love approach'd me under Friendship's name;
My fancy form'd thee of angelic kind,
Some emanation of th' all-beauteous Mind.
Those smiling eyes, attemp'ring ev'ry ray,
Shone sweetly lambent with celestial day.
Guiltless I gaz'd; Heav'n listen'd while you sung;
And truths divine came mended from that tongue.
From lips like those what precept fail'd to move?
Too soon they taught me 'twas no sin to love:
Back thro' the paths of pleasing sense I ran,
Nor wish'd an Angel whom I lov'd a Man.
Dim and remote the joys of saints I see;
Nor envy them that heav'n I lose for thee.
  How oft, when press'd to marriage, have I said,
Curse on all laws but those which love has made?
Love, free as air, at sight of human ties,
Spreads his light wings, and in a moment flies.

Let wealth, let honour, wait the wedded dame,
August her deed, and sacred be her fame;
Before true passion all those views remove,
Fame, wealth, and honour! what are you to Love?
The jealous God, when we profane His fires,
Those restless passions in revenge inspires,
And bids them make mistaken mortals groan,
Who seek in love for aught but love alone.
Should at my feet the world's great Master fall,
Himself, His throne, His world, I'd scorn 'em all:
Not Cæsar's empress would I deign to prove;
No, make me mistress to the man I love;
If there be yet another name more free,
More fond than mistress, make me that to thee!
Oh! happy state! when souls each other draw,
When love is liberty, and nature law:
All then is full, possessing and possess'd,
No craving void left aching in the breast:
Ev'n thought meets thought, ere from the lips it part,
And each warm wish springs mutual from the heart.
This sure is bliss (if bliss on earth there be),
And once the lot of Abelard and me.
Alas, how chang'd! what sudden horrors rise!
A naked Lover bound and bleeding lies!
Where, where was Eloïse! her voice, her hand,
Her poniard, had oppos'd the dire command.
Barbarian, stay! that bloody stroke restrain;
The crime was common, common be the pain.
I can no more; by shame, by rage suppress'd,
Let tears, and burning blushes speak the rest.
  Canst thou forget that sad, that solemn day,
When victims at yon altar's foot we lay?
Canst thou forget what tears that moment fell,
When, warm in youth, I bade the world farewell?
As with cold lips I kiss'd the sacred veil,
The shrines all trembled, and the lamps grew pale:
Heav'n scarce believ'd the Conquest it survey'd,
And Saints with wonder heard the vows I made,
Yet then, to those dread altars as I drew,
Not on the Cross my eyes were fix'd, but you:
Not grace, or zeal, love only was my call,
And if I lose thy love, I lose my all.

Come! with thy looks, thy words, relieve my woe; 1
Those still at least are left thee to bestow.
Still on thy breast enamour'd let me lie,
Still drink delicious poison from thy eye,
Pant on thy lip, and to thy heart be press'd;
Give all thou canst—and let me dream the rest.
Ah no! instruct me other joys to prize,
With other beauties charm my partial eyes,
Full in my view set all the bright abode,
And make my soul quit Abelard for God.
  Ah, think at least thy flock deserves thy care,
Plants of thy hand, and children of thy pray'r.
From the false world in early youth they fled,
By thee to mountains, wilds, and deserts led.
You rais'd these hallow'd walls; the desert smil'd,
And Paradise was open'd in the Wild. p. 102
No weeping orphan saw his father's stores
Our shrines irradiate, or emblaze the floors;
No silver saints, by dying misers giv'n,
Here brib'd the rage of ill-requited Heav'n:
But such plain roofs as Piety could raise,
And only vocal with the Maker's praise.
In these lone walls (their days eternal bound)
These moss-grown domes with spiry turrets crown'd,
Where awful arches make a noon-day night,
And the dim windows shed a solemn light;
Thy eyes diffus'd a reconciling ray,
And gleams of glory brighten'd all the day.
But now no face divine contentment wears,
'Tis all blank sadness, or continual tears.
See how the force of others' pray'rs I try
(O pious fraud of am'rous charity!),
But why should I on others' pray'rs depend?
Come thou, my father, brother, husband, friend!
Ah let thy handmaid, sister, daughter move,
And all those tender names in one, thy love!
The darksome pines that o'er yon rocks reclin'd
Wave high, and murmur to the hollow wind,
The wand'ring streams that shine between the hills,
The grots that echo to the tinkling rills,
The dying gales that pant upon the trees,
The lakes that quiver to the curling breeze;

No more these scenes my meditation aid,
Or lull to rest the visionary maid.
But o'er the twilight groves and dusky caves,
Long-sounding aisles, and intermingled graves,
Black Melancholy sits, and round her throws
A death-like silence, and a dead repose:
Her gloomy presence saddens all the scene,
Shades ev'ry flow'r, and darkens ev'ry green,
Deepens the murmur of the falling floods,
And breathes a browner horror on the woods.
 Yet here for ever, ever must I stay;
Sad proof how well a lover can obey!
Death, only death, can break the lasting chain:
And here, ev'n then, shall my cold dust remain,
Here all its frailties, all its flames resign,
And wait till 'tis no sin to mix with thine,
 Ah wretch! believ'd the spouse of God in vain,
Confess'd within the slave of love and man.
Assist me, Heav'n! but whence arose that pray'r?
Sprung it from piety, or from despair?
Ev'n here, where frozen chastity retires,
Love finds an altar for forbidden fires.
I ought to grieve, but cannot what I ought;
I mourn the lover, not lament the fault;
I view my crime, but kindle at the view,
Repent old pleasures, and solicit new;
Now turn'd to Heav'n, I weep my past offence,
Now think of thee, and curse my innocence.
Of all affliction taught a lover yet,
'Tis sure the hardest science to forget!
How shall I lose the sin, yet keep the sense,
And love th' offender, yet detest th' offence?
How the dear object from the crime remove,
Or how distinguish penitence from love?
Unequal task! a passion to resign,
For hearts so touch'd, so pierc'd, so lost as mine.
Ere such a soul regains its peaceful state,
How often must it love, how often hate!
How often hope, despair, resent, regret,
Conceal, disdain,—do all things but forget.
But let Heav'n seize it, all at once 'tis fir'd;
Not touch'd, but rapt; not waken'd, but inspir'd!

Oh come? oh teach me nature to subdue,
Renounce my love, my life, myself—and you.
Fill my fond heart with God alone, for He
Alone can rival, can succeed to thee.
 How happy is the blameless Vestal's lot!
The world forgetting, by the world forgot:
Eternal sunshine of the spotless mind!
Each pray'r accepted, and each wish resign'd;
Labour and rest, that equal periods keep;
Obedient slumbers that can wake and weep; '
Desires compos'd, affections ever ev'n;
Tears that delight, and sighs that waft to Heav'n.
Grace shines around her with serenest beams,
And whisp'ring Angels prompt her golden dreams.
For her th' unfading rose of Eden blooms,
And wings of Seraphs shed divine perfumes,
For her the Spouse prepares the bridal ring,
For her white virgins Hymenæals sing,
To sounds of heav'nly harps she dies away,
And melts in visions of eternal day.
 Far other dreams my erring soul employ,
Far other raptures, of unholy joy:
When at the close of each sad, sorrowing day,
Fancy restores what vengeance snatch'd away,
Then conscience sleeps, and leaving nature free,
All my loose soul unbounded springs to thee.
O Burst, dear horrors of all-conscious night;
How glowing guilt exalts the keen delight!
Provoking Dæmons all restraint remove,
And stir within me ev'ry source of love.
I hear thee, view thee, gaze o'er all thy charms,
And round thy phantom glue my clasping arms.
I wake:—no more I hear, no more I view,
The phantom flies me, as unkind as you.
I call aloud; it hears not what I say:
I stretch my empty arms; it glides away.
To dream once more I close my willing eyes;
Ye soft illusions, dear deceits, arise!
Alas, no more! methinks we wand'ring go
Thro' dreary wastes, and weep each other's woe,
Where round some mould ring tow'r pale ivy creeps,
And low-brow'd rocks hang nodding o'er the deeps.

Sudden you mount, you beckon from the skies;
Clouds interpose, waves roar, and winds arise.
I shriek, start up, the same sad prospect find,
And wake to all the griefs I left behind.
  For thee the fates, severely kind, ordain
A cool suspense from pleasure and from pain;
Thy life a long dead calm of fix'd repose;
No pulse that riots, and no blood that glows.
Still as the sea, ere winds were taught to blow,
Or moving spirit bade the waters flow;
Soft as the slumbers of a saint forgiv'n,
And mild as op'ning gleams of promis'd heav'n.
  Come, Abelard! for what hast thou to dread?
The torch of Venus burns not for the dead.
Nature stands check'd; Religion disapproves;
Ev'n thou art cold—yet Eloïsa loves.
Ah hopeless, lasting flames! like those that burn
To light the dead, and warm the unfruitful urn.
  What scenes appear where'er I turn my view?
The dear Ideas, where I fly, pursue,
Rise in the grove, before the altar rise,
Stain all my soul, and wanton in my eyes.
I waste the Matin lamp in sighs for thee,
Thy image steals between my God and me,
Thy voice I seem in ev'ry hymn to hear,
With ev'ry bead I drop too soft a tear.
When from the censer clouds of fragrance roll,
And swelling organs lift the rising soul,
One thought of thee puts all the pomp to flight,
Priests, tapers, temples, swim before my sight:
In seas of flame my plunging soul is drown'd,
While Altars blaze, and Angels tremble round
  While prostrate here in humble grief I lie,
Kind, virtuous drops just gath'ring in my eye,
While praying, trembling, in the dust I roll,
And dawning grace is op'ning on my soul:
Come, if thou dar'st, all charming as thou art!
Oppose thyself to Heav'n; dispute my heart;
Come, with one glance of those deluding eyes
Blot out each bright Idea of the skies;
Take back that grace, those sorrows, and those tears;
Take back my fruitless penitence and pray'rs;

Snatch me, just mounting, from the blest abode;
Assist the fiends, and tear me from my God!
  No, fly me, fly me, far as Pole from Pole;
Rise Alps between us! and whole oceans roll!
Ah, come not, write not, think not once of me,
Nor share one pang of all I felt for thee.
Thy oaths I quit, thy memory resign;
Forget, renounce me, hate whate'er was mine.
Fair eyes, and tempting looks (which yet I view!),
Long lov'd, ador'd ideas, all adieu!
O Grace serene! O Virtue heav'nly fair!
Divine oblivion of low-thoughted care!
Fresh blooming Hope, gay daughter of the sky!
And Faith, our early immortality!
Enter, each mild, each amicable guest!
Receive, and wrap me in eternal rest:
  See in her cell sad Eloïsa spread,
Propt on some tomb, a neighbour of the dead.
In each low wind methinks a Spirit calls,
And more than Echoes talk along the walls.
Here, as I watch'd the dying lamps around,
From yonder shrine I heard a hollow sound.
'Come, sister, come!' (it said, or seem'd to say)
'Thy place is here, sad sister, come away!
Once like thyself, I trembled, wept, and pray'd,
Love's victim then, tho' now a sainted maid:
But all is calm in this eternal sleep;
Here grief forgets to groan, and love to weep,
Ev'n superstition loses ev'ry fear:
For God, not man, absolves our frailties here.'
  I come, I come! prepare your roseate bow'rs,
Celestial palms, and ever-blooming flow'rs.
Thither, where sinners may have rest, I go,
Where flames refin'd in breasts seraphic glow;
Thou, Abelard! the last sad office pay,
And smooth my passage to the realms of day;
See my lips tremble, and my eyeballs roll,
Suck my last breath, and catch my flying soul!
Ah no—in sacred vestments may'st thou stand,
The hallow'd taper trembling in thy hand,
Present the Cross before my lifted eye,
Teach me at once, and learn of me to die.

Ah then, thy once-lov'd Eloïsa see!
  It will be then no crime to gaze on me.
See from my cheek the transient roses fly!
See the last sparkle languish in my eye!
'Till ev'ry motion, pulse, and breath be o'er;
And ev'n my Abelard be lov'd no more.
O Death all-eloquent! you only prove
What dust we dote on when 'tis man we love.
  Then too, when fate shall thy fair frame destroy
(That cause of all my guilt, and all my joy),
In trance ecstatic may thy pangs be drown'd,
Bright clouds descend, and Angels watch thee round,
From op'ning skies may streaming glories shine,
And saints embrace thee with a love like mine.
  May one kind grave unite each hapless name,
And graft my love immortal on thy fame!
Then, ages hence, when all my woes are o'er,
When this rebellious heart shall beat no more;
If ever chance two wand'ring lovers brings
To Paraclete's white walls and silver springs,
O'er the pale marble shall they join their heads,
And drink the falling tears each other sheds;
Then sadly say, with mutual pity mov'd,
'Oh may we never love as these have lov'd!'
From the full choir when loud Hosannas rise,
And swell the pomp of dreadful sacrifice,
Amid that scene if some relenting eye
Glance on the stone where our cold relics lie,
Devotion's self shall steal a thought from Heav'n,
One human tear shall drop and be forgiv'n.
And sure, if fate some future bard shall join
In sad similitude of griefs to mine,
Condemn'd whole years in absence to deplore,
And image charms he must behold no more;
Such, if there be, who loves so long, so well;
Let him our sad, our tender story tell;
The well-sung woes will soothe my pensive ghost;
He best can paint 'em who shall feel 'em most.

28988269R00038

Made in the USA
San Bernardino, CA
11 January 2016